Literacy and the New Work Order

An international literature review

WITHDRAWN

Literacy and the New Work Order

An international literature review

by Chris Holland
with Fiona Frank and Tony Cooke

Published by the National Institute of Adult Continuing Education
(England and Wales)

Renaissance House, 20 Princess Road West, Leicester LE1 6TP

Company registration no. 2603322
Charity registration no. 1002775

First published 1998, Reprinted 2003
© NIACE

CATALOGUING IN PUBLICATION DATA
A CIP record for this title is available from the British Library
ISBN 1 86201 008 0

Typeset by The Midlands Book Typesetting Company
Cover design by Boldface
Printed & bound by Antony Rowe Ltd, Eastbourne

About the authors

CHRIS HOLLAND
Chris Holland is a Workplace Literacy Consultant, working with the Centre for the Study of Education and Training at Lancaster University (UK) during 1996 and UNITEC, Auckland (NZ) during 1997 to complete this review. In New Zealand, Chris has been involved for many years as a practitioner and researcher in education for employed and unemployed workers. In 1994 she won a Commonwealth Relations Trust bursary to research workplace education in the UK. Thus she was able to develop an international dimension to her work, becoming increasingly interested in the global politics of workplace literacy. Chris was responsible for the selection, reading and analysis of texts, setting up a consultative committee of writers and practitioners in the field, and writing the review. Chris has brought her experience to the development of accredited tutor training in workplace education, and is currently engaged in delivering this training to FE colleges.

FIONA FRANK
Fiona Frank has been based at CSET, the Centre for the Study of Education and Training at Lancaster University, since 1991. She has carried out a Leverhulme Trust funded research project on workplace basic skills programmes (Frank and Hamilton, 1993) and a five-year follow-up study tracking 18 learners who had taken workplace basic skills programmes in 1991 and 1992 (Frank, 1996). She founded the (UK) Workplace Basic Skills Training Network in 1993. Since 1996 she has also been Project Consultant with Lancaster Employee Development Consortium.
Fiona conceived the initial idea for this book, and organised the funding for Chris to do the first six months of the research in the UK in 1996. She had an editorial input in the final stages of the project.

TONY COOKE
Tony Cooke lives in Lancaster and has always been involved in working closely with community groups and organisations, helping to represent the interests of disabled people and, in particular, those with mental health problems. He has worked with Lancaster University, the Adult College, Lancaster, Social Services, Health Authorities and sundry voluntary organisations. He is also a working musician.

Acknowledgements

This book was jointly funded by NIACE and Lancaster University Social Science Faculty Research Fund, and supported by UNITEC in New Zealand. I wish to extend my thanks to the Centre for the Study of Education and Training at Lancaster University for providing the UK contract to support this undertaking, and to UNITEC (NZ) who allowed me some time under my teaching contract for its completion in New Zealand. I received technological assistance from Auckland University, without which the work would have been extremely difficult.

I am grateful to the initial funders, NIACE, and, in particular, Christopher Feeney and, later, Virman Man for their confidence in the project and for their commitment to the publication of this review.

The idea for this book was conceived by Fiona Frank, Research Associate at CSET, the Centre for the Study of Education and Training, Lancaster University. I wish to acknowledge Fiona's vision and persistent confidence. I appreciate, also, her efforts in negotiating funding and publication with NIACE. I am grateful for her continuing arrangement of resources in the UK and in New Zealand and for her encouragement throughout.

I want to thank Tony Cooke for his complete patience, extensive proof reading and correction of drafts, searching of incomplete references, and for challenging discussions of the issues surrounding workplace education.

Thanks go to the Consultative Committee, who are: Jane Mace, Brian Street, Mary Hamilton, David Barton, Catherine Macrae (UK), Sheryl Gowen, Glynda Hull, James Paul Gee, Paul Jurmo (USA), Colin Lankshear, Peter O'Connor (Australia), Richard Darville (Canada) and John Benseman (New Zealand). Members of this committee have contributed a great deal to this project.

Finally, library staff at UNITEC and Lancaster University have been especially courteous and forbearing, going out of their way to assist me to locate hard-to-find texts.

CHRIS HOLLAND

Contents

Foreword

During the past 15 years or so literacy has undergone a major identity and status change. Prior to that, 'literacy' had been very much a linguistic marker of marginal spaces, used mainly in association with 'marginal' people' ('illiterates'). Recently it has been elevated to the status of a lofty mainstream educational ideal in various constructions of 'higher order literacy'.

Literacy and The New Work Order is a timely, appropriate, thoughtful, and thought-provoking resource. It is very much a product of its times: modelling as it does the very kind of meta-analysis so trumpeted by champions of the new capitalism and its new work order. Unlike the work of those who champion the new work order, however, Chris Holland invites us explicitly to pursue a critically informed perspective on the new work order and its relationships with literacies.

At a time when so many invitations are purely formal, leaving it to people to pick their own ways across 'level playing fields' of economic, social and cultural life, the present author backs her invitation with something which has genuine substance: a useful and usable resource.

I wholeheartedly endorse this book, *Literacy and the New Work Order*, and look forward to enjoying some of the fruits it bears.

Professor Colin Lankshear, Queensland University of Technology, 1997.

Introduction

by Professor Colin Lankshear

Today, the term 'literacy' spans a very wide spectrum of meanings. Some remain close to its earlier connotative and denotative associations – such as in lingering constructions of basic, functional, and remedial literacy. Others, however, expand to take in sophisticated levels of analysis, abstraction, symbol manipulation, and theoretical knowledge and applications. These are the so-called 'higher order literacies' within (especially) mathematics, science and technology. They are associated with the shift in educational reform away from 'basics' and toward 'excellence' – where excellence is defined in terms of higher levels and standards of achievement, with a strong emphasis on 'meta-level' understandings and appropriations (Gee 1996). This emphasis is apparent everywhere in current discursive constructions of literacy (DEET 1991a, 1991b; Kirsch et al 1993; National Commission for Excellence in Education 1983; Toch 1991; US Congress 1994; US Congress, Office of Technology Assessment 1993).

We probably cannot overestimate the extent to which educational reform since the early 1980s has been a response to 'the economic imperative'. Analysts of educational reform in Anglo-American countries typically describe reform initiatives as responses to three interrelated concerns: (1) revitalizing economic competitiveness and advantage; (2) maintaining a 'viable' degree of cultural coherence and cohesion, whilst orchestrating 'necessary' institutional change with an eye to the future; (3) preserving a sense of nationhood, and national allegiance and solidarity in the face of escalating cultural and ethnic diversity within national borders, intensified international and transnational forms of organisation, experience and interchange, and postmodern celebrations of individuality with consequent erosion of more collective forms of identity.

Of these, say Toch (1991:17), with particular reference to the US, the 'quest for renewed economic competitiveness' was 'the principal reason that the nation supported the push for excellence in education so strongly; more than anything else, it was the competitiveness theme that defined the education crisis in the nation's eyes'. This emphasis is writ large in dominant current conceptions and practices of literacy in Britain, North America and Australasia, although the specific examples I will draw on here are mainly from the US and Australia.

I discern a broad typology of four prevalent 'official' constructions of literacy in countries like our own at present. Moreover, I have argued elsewhere (Lankshear 1997) that these constructions are unfolding in tandem with an evolving 'new work order' (Gee, Hull and Lankshear 1996). Let me deal with these briefly in turn, as a way of situating the important work undertaken by Chris Holland in the present volume.

The 'lingering basics': Recovering 'marginals' for baseline incorporation

Literacy as mastery of fundamentals of encoding and decoding print texts (including elementary math operations) has an ambiguous position within reform discourse. On one hand, it is believed that survival level reading and writing competencies are no longer enough for effective participation in the economic and social mainstream. *A Nation at Risk* laments (National Commission for Excellence in Education 1983: 14) that 'in some metropolitan areas basic literacy has become the goal rather than the starting point'. On the other hand, it is acknowledged emphatically that integration into public life demands, minimally, the ability to negotiate texts encountered in the course of everyday routines. A 1993 US report cites statistics claiming that 21–23% – or between 40 and 44 million US adults – would perform at the lowest level of prose, document, and quantitative proficiencies on the test used: ranging from those who could perform few or no items at all on the test, to those who could not perform above this level (Kirsch *et al* 1993: xiv). *Goals 2000* pledges more adult literacy programs to help improve 'the ties between home and school, and enhance parents' work and home lives' (US Congress 1994: Goal 6, B (iv)).

Reform initiatives address basic and functional literacy competencies at both school and adult education levels, although the constructions differ between these levels. At school level basic literacy is framed in terms of mastering the building blocks of code breaking: knowing the alphabetic script visually and phonetically, and grasping the mechanism of putting elements of the script together to encode or decode words, and to separate words or add them together to read and write sentences. Either, meaning is assumed to reside in the words such that fluent basic textual skills will result in comprehension, or else comprehension is regarded as a distinct skill which 'builds on' literacy and is taught separately, albeit in conjunction, with literacy. Remedial literacy programs focus on accuracy and self-correction in reading aloud exercises, and correct spelling in written work. Remedial students are subjected to batteries of word and dictation activities and tests, as well as exercises concerned with letter identification and concepts about print. Teachers are required to maintain accurate and comprehensive records for diagnosis, validation, and accountability purposes.

At the adult level, basic literacy is defined in terms of baseline functional competencies, or 'life skills' (US Congress, Office of Technology Assessment

1993: 32) all adults should have. These comprise ability 'to perform specific literacy-related tasks in the context of work, family and other 'real-life' situations'. Often, competency is translated into 'individualized sets of requisite skills' to take account of individual differences in life circumstances. In the test mentioned above, basic literacy is operationalised in terms of prose, document and quantitative proficiency at the bottom levels. For example, Level 1 Prose proficiency tasks include identifying a country in a short article, and locating one piece of information in a sports article. Level 2 tasks include locating two pieces of information from a sports article, and interpreting instructions from an appliance warranty. Document proficiency tasks at Level 1 include signing one's name, and locating the expiry date on a driver's license; and, at Level 2, locating an intersection on a street map, and identifying and entering information on an application for a social security card. Quantitative proficiency task examples at Level 1 include totalling a bank deposit entry and, at Level 2, calculating total costs of a purchase on an order form, and determining the difference in price between tickets for two shows.

Whereas basic literacy competence for school learners relates to mastery of generalisable techniques and concepts that are presumed to be building blocks for subsequent education – decontextualised tools to serve as means for accessing subsequent content and higher order skills – the case seems different with adults. Adult basic and functional literacy competence consists more in the completion of immediate tasks which are their own ends, and which are directly and functionally related to daily survival needs.

The 'new basics': Applied language, problem-solving and 'critical' thinking

A central motif in educational reform discourse is that the 'old basics' are no longer sufficient for effective participation in modern societies. The qualitative shifts in social practices variously associated with transition from an agri-industrial economy to a post-industrial information/services economy; from 'fordism' to 'post-fordism'; from more personal face-to-face communities to impersonal metropolitan and, even, virtual communities; from a paternal (welfare) state to a more devolved state requiring greater self-sufficiency, and so on; are seen to call for qualitatively more sophisticated ('smart'), abstract, symbolic-logical capacities than were needed in the past. Some see this in terms of a generalised shift toward a more 'meta-level' modus operandi, captured in emphases on higher order skills as the norm. In this context, it is argued, the old 'base' needs to be raised. This sentiment is captured in statements like

'Many 17-year-olds do not possess the 'higher order' intellectual skills we should expect of them. Nearly 40% cannot draw inferences from written material; only

one-fifth can write a persuasive essay; and only one-third an solve a mathematics problem requiring several steps'. (A Nation at Risk,p.9).

'Some worry that schools may emphasize such rudiments as reading and computation at the expense of other essential skills such as comprehension, analysis, solving problems, and drawing conclusions'. (A Nation at Risk, p. 9).

'The percentage of all students who demonstrate ability to reason, solve problems, apply knowledge, and write and communicate effectively will increase substantially'. (Goals 2000, Goal 3 B (ii)).

'The new jobs demanded more than mastery of basic reading, writing, and arithmetic. They called for workers with 'thinking skills', with the ability to master new knowledge on the job. 'In the future' said Theodore Sizer in Horace's Compromise . . . "The best vocational education will be one in general education in the use of one's mind" '. (Toch 1991: 40).

The generic term, 'critical thinking', is often used as a grab bag for such higher order skills as comprehension, problem solving and analysis, and conjoined with reading, writing, speaking, listening – or, in short, 'communications' – to encapsulate the 'new basic literacy'. Maxson and Hair (1991: 1), for example, frame their conception of critical literacy in just this way, stating: 'Critical literacy, a relatively new term, combines the concepts of critical thinking and communications'.

In similar vein, *Australia's Language: The Australian Language and Literacy Policy* (DEET 1991a), identifies 'effective literacy' for all Australians as its primary objective. 'The first goal of the policy is for all Australians to develop and maintain effective literacy in English to enable them to participate in Australian society' (p.4). Effective literacy is defined as 'intrinsically purposeful, flexible and dynamic and involves the integration of speaking, listening, and critical thinking with reading and writing' (p. 5), and 'continues to develop throughout an individual's lifetime' (1991b: 9), with 'the support of education and training programs'. This is very different from the 'old basic literacy' as described above, although it retains the notion of 'a base' from which further and ongoing development occurs with the assistance of 'programs'.

These constructions remain abstract until they are put into explicit contexts. As might be expected, concrete embodiments are provided most regularly and graphically in terms of life on the floor of the new times workplace: with its demands for team work (requiring 'communications skills'), self-direction (calling for 'problem-solving' and 'trouble shooting' capacities), and devolved responsibility throughout the entire enterprise for producing the efficiency and competitive edge (abilities to 'innovate', 'maintain quality', 'continually improve') that enhances the success of the enterprise and, to that extent, improves workers' prospects of job security. In the words of Motorola's corporate vice-president for training and education:

'Ten years ago we hired people to perform tasks and didn't ask them to do a lot of thinking. If a machine went down, workers raised their hands and a trouble shooter came to fix it . . . Then all the rules of manufacturing and competition changed . . . We learned that line workers had to actually understand their work and their equipment . . . that change had to be continuous and participative . . . From the kind of skill instruction we envisioned at the outset, we moved out in both directions: down, toward grade school basics as fundamental as the three Rs; up, toward new concepts of work, quality, community, learning, and leadership . . . Today we expect workers to know their equipment and to begin any troubleshooting process themselves . . . they have to be able to analyze problems and then communicate them.' (Wiggenhorn 1990: 71–72)

'Elite literacies': Higher order scientific, technological, and symbolic literacies

At the heart of the 'education for excellence' reform discourse are the two core beliefs that post-elementary education should emphasize academic learning, and that academic subject standards should be greatly increased (Toch 1991:1). At a conjuncture when 'Knowledge, learning, information, and skilled intelligence are the new raw materials of international commerce' (National Commission for Excellence in Education 1983: 7), 'our once unchallenged preeminence in commerce, industry, science, and technological innovation is being overtaken by competitors throughout the world (*ibid*: 5). A 1984 National Academy of Sciences task force insisted (1984: xi) that 'those who enter the workforce after earning a high school diploma need virtually the same competencies as those going on to college'. This is reflected in *Goals 2000*, where Goal 6 objective (v) states that the proportion of college graduates who demonstrate an advanced ability to think critically, communicate effectively, and solve problems will increase substantially: where the qualifier 'advanced' marks the only significant difference from Goal 3 objective (ii), cited above.

'Elite literacies' comprise high level mastery of subject or discipline literacies, understood in terms of their respective 'languages' and 'literatures' (cf, Hirst 1974). The language of an academic subject/discipline is basically the 'logic' and process of inquiry within that field. It consists of the specialised concepts, tests, and procedures employed in doing, for example, science or history, and their organisation into an overall structure (eg, to appreciate how the litmus test in chemistry relates to aspects of experimental design, the taxonomy of acids and alkalis, etc). The literature of a subject/discipline consists of the content of work in the field – the accumulated attainments of people working in the field, who have brought its language to bear on its existing literature in order to extend knowledge, understanding, theory, and applications within everyday life.

Command of both the language and literature of a field of inquiry permits critique, innovation, variation, diversification, refinement, and so on, to occur. These may range from producing entirely new approaches to managing organisations, or new kinds of computer hardware and software (from mainframe to PC; DOS to Windows, addition of sound and video), to producing new reporting processes for literacy attainment and new ways of conceiving literacy; from variations within architectural and engineering design, to variations on mass produced commodities which provide a semblance of individuality or novelty.

This is very much the literacy of what Robert Reich (1992) calls 'symbolic analysis', and Peter Drucker (1993) calls 'knowledge work'. This work is seen as the real 'value-adding' work within modern economies. The scientist, historian, architect, software designer, composer, management theorist, and electronic engineer, all manipulate, modify, refine, combine, and in other ways employ symbols contained in or derived from the language and literature of their disciplines to produce new knowledge, innovative designs, new applications of theory, and so on. These can be drawn on to 'add maximum value' to raw materials and labour in the process of producing goods and services. Increasingly, the critical dimension of knowledge work is valued mainly, if not solely, in terms of value-adding economic potential. It is critical analysis and critical judgment directed toward innovation and improvement within the parameters of a field or enterprise, rather than criticism in larger terms which might hold the field and its applications and effects, or an enterprise and its goals, up to scrutiny.

The emphasis and value attached to these elite literacies is a consequence of the fact that high impact innovation comes from the application of theoretical knowledge. Whereas the new industries of the last century, such as 'electricity, steel, the telephone and automobile . . . were invented by 'talented tinkerers' (Bell 1974) rather than through applications of scientific theory', the big impact inventions of this century, like 'the computer, jet aircraft, laser surgery, the birth control pill, the social survey . . . and their many derivations and application, come from theory-driven scientific laboratories' (Levett and Lankshear 1990: 4).

Foreign language literacy: proficiency for global dealings?

Following decades of decline in percentages of students learning a foreign language in schools, colleges and universities (DEET 1991a: 15; Toch 1991: 8), reform discourse has given renewed attention to increasing second language proficiency.

Justifications advanced in policy documents and supporting texts often foreground 'humanist' considerations in support of foreign language proficiency and bilingualism: whether by increasing foreign language enrolments, or by maintaining community languages and ensuring ESL proficiency among linguistic minority groups. Sooner or later, however, economic motives generally emerge as the real reasons behind efforts to promote foreign language proficiency. *Australia's Language* gives as its first reason the fact that it enriches our community intellectually, educationally and culturally; and second, that it contributes to economic, diplomatic, strategic, scientific and technological development (DEET 1991b: 14–15). However, Australia's location in the Asia-Pacific region and its patterns of overseas trade are the only relevant factor explicitly mentioned with respect to developing a strategy which '[strikes] a balance between the diversity of languages which could be taught and the limits of resources that are available' (*ibid*: 15).

Elsewhere, influential statements are direct and unambiguous: for example, US Senator Paul Simon's reference to tongue-tied Americans trying to do business across the globe, in a world where there are 10,000 leading Japanese business persons speaking English to less than 1,000 Americans, and where 'you can buy in any language, but sell only in the customer's' (Kearns and Doyle 1991: 87).

Two main factors have generated the emergence of second language literacy education as a new (and pressing) capitalist instrumentality. First, trading partners have changed greatly for Anglophone economies, and many of our new partners have not been exposed to decades (or centuries) of colonial or neo-colonial English language hegemony. Second, trade competition has become intense. Many countries now produce commodities previously produced by relatively few. Within this context of intensified competition, the capacity to market, sell, inform, and provide after sales support in the customer's language becomes a crucial element of competitive edge.

How is 'proficiency' constructed? *Goals 2000* claims only that by the year 2000 'the percentage of students who are competent in more than one language will increase substantially' (Goal 3 B (v)). *A Nation at Risk* (p. 26) offers more substantial, if tacit, clues. In quantitative terms, proficiency in a foreign language is seen to require 'from 4 to 6 years of study', and is desirable because it 'introduces students to non-English speaking cultures, heightens awareness and comprehension of one's native tongue, and serves the Nation's needs in commerce, diplomacy, defense, and education'. This suggests that the baseline for proficiency is communicative competence which allows functional cross-cultural access to a range of discursive practices. 'Full proficiency' would, presumably, involve combinations of fluency and cultural awareness equal to being persuasive, diplomatic and strategic, in sensitive and potentially high risk or high gain situations.

Reflections

If this typology of 'official' literacy constructions is accurate, there is much we should be troubled about in the contemporary literacy scene. It might be argued that the four literacies described here constitute, in effect, a new word order, to which individuals and groups will have differential access. It seems likely, also, that where individuals end up in the new word order will be related in material ways to their prospects within the new work order. Crucial issues of equality, social justice, inclusivity and the like are at stake here – although there remains a massive amount of empirical work to be done if we are to understand the various micro and macro processes operating daily around literacy, education, and work in ways that clarify whatever relationship exists between new orders of word and work. If, however, some kind of functional symmetry does operate between a new word order and the new work order, we should want to know as much about it as we can, and to act politically and educationally on that knowledge.

Other apparent trends are worthy of our concern as well. The economisation of literacy has meant that within multi-language societies 'literacy' has effectively come to mean 'standard English literacy' – with concomitant implications for speaker-writers of minority dialects of English and languages other than English, for cultural 'validity', and so on. At another level, we are presently caught up in a general clamour to technologise literacy, as the price to be paid for meeting the production and consumption 'needs' of an increasingly global informational economy (Carnoy et al 1993). Furthermore, under the current 'competency-based everything' regime, literacies are subject to powerful forces of 'standardisation' and 'homogenisation'. At the same time, the economic 'imperative' tends to individualise and commodify literacy in worrying ways. This latter trend bears closer examination.

Despite increased emphasis within work and civic domains on team work and participation in communities of practice, literacy is seen to consist in the measured capacities of the individual learner. This 'literacy' is then compiled into personal portfolios. At a time when individuals must be prepared to move around to find employment, 'portable certified literacy competence' assumes functional significance.

This is a facet of 'possessive individualism', a key operating principle of current reform discourse, and grounded in a liberal conception of people and society, according to which: 'society is composed of free, equal individuals who are related to each other as proprietors of their own capabilities. Their successes and acquisitions are the products of their own initiatives, and it is the role of institutions to foster and support their personal development' – not least because national revitalisation – economic, cultural, and civic – will 'result from the good works of individuals' (Popkewitz 1991: 150).

At the same time, literacy is profoundly commodified within the current reform agenda, in relation to assessment, and evaluation packages, validation packages, remedial teaching packages, packaged standards, profiles, and curriculum guidelines, textbook packages, and teacher professional development packages promising recipes and resources for securing the required performance outcomes.

Finally, the current literacy agenda of educational reform can be seen as 'incorporating' critique in ways that should concern supporters of expansive and democratic approaches to education. Although educational reform discourse emphasises critical forms of literate practice, couched in terms of a 'critical thinking' component of effective literacy, or as text-mediated acts of problem solving, it is important to recognise the nature and limits of the critical literacies proposed. They are typically practices which permit subjecting means to critique, but take ends as given. References to critical literacy, critical analysis, critical thinking, problem solving, and the like, have, 'in the current climate . . . a mixture of references to functional or useful knowledge that relates to demands of the economy and labor formation, as well as more general claims about social inquiry and innovation' (Popkewitz 1991: 128).

The nearer that literacy approaches the world beyond school, the more functional and instrumental critique becomes, with emphasis on finding new and better ways of meeting institutional targets (of quality, productivity, innovation, improvement), but where these targets are themselves beyond question. The logic here parallels that described by Delgado-Gaitan (1990: 2) as operating in notions of empowerment construed as 'the act of showing people how to work within a system from the perspective of people in power'.

The fact that standards are specified so tightly and rigidly within the current reform agenda reveals that the ends driving these standards are to be taken as beyond critique.

Plainly, there is much to think about at the confluence of literacy and work. There is a massive literature in this area. Actually, there are massive literatures in the area, with some important differences among them. Issues at stake around these differences may easily escape us. In this regard, an analytical annotated review of relevant literature becomes an extremely useful resource, as well as being a good idea.

References

Bell, D. (1974). *The Coming of Post Industrial Society: A Venture in Social Forecasting*. London: Heinemann.

Carnoy, M., Castells, M., Cohen, S. and Cardoso, F.H. (1993). *The New Global Economy in the Information Age: Reflections on our Changing World*. University Park, PA: The Pennsylvania State University Press.

Department of Employment, Education, and Training (1991a). *Australia's language: The Australian Language and Literacy Policy – The Policy Paper*. Canberra: Australian Government Publishing Service.

Department of Employment, Education and Training (1991b). *Australia's language: The Australian Language and Literacy Policy – Companion volume to the policy paper*. Canberra: Australian Government Publishing Service.

Delgado-Gaitan, C. (1990). *Literacy for empowerment*. London: Falmer Press.

Drucker, P. (1993). *Post-capitalist society*. New York: Harper.

Gee, J.P. (1996). *Social Linguistics and Literacies: Ideology in Discourses*. London: Taylor and Francis. 2nd edition.

Gee, J.P., Hull, G. And Lankshear, C. (1996). *The New Work Order: Behind the language of the new capitalism*. Sydney and Boulder Colorado: Allen and Unwin and Westview Press.

Hirst, P. (1974). *Knowledge and the curriculum*. London: Routledge and Kegan Paul.

Kearns, D. and Doyle, D. (1991). *Winning the Brain Race: A Bold Plan to Make our Schools Competitive*. San Francisco: ICS Press.

Kirsch, I. et al (1993). *Adult literacy in America: A first look at the results of the National Adult Literacy Survey*. Washington, DC: US Department of Education, Office of Educational Research and Improvement.

Lankshear, C. (1997). Language and the New Capitalism. *The International Journal of Inclusive Education* 1, 3 (in press)

Levett, A. and Lankshear, C. (1990). *Going for Gold: Priorities for Schooling in the Nineties*. Wellington: Brasell Press.

Maxson, J. and Hair, B. (1990). *Managing diversity: A key to building a quality workforce*. Columbus: National Alliance of Community and TechnicalColleges.

National Academy of Science Task Force (1984). *High Schools and the Changing Workplace: The Employers' View*. Washington DC: National Academy Press.

National Commission on Excellence in Education (1983). *A Nation at Risk. The Imperative for Educational Reform*. Washington DC: US Department of Education.

Popkewitz, T. (1991). *A Political Sociology of Educational Reform: Power/ knowledge in Teaching, Teacher Education, and Research*. New York:Teachers College Press.

Reich, R. (1992). *The Work of Nations*. New York: Vintage Books.

Toch, T. (1991). *In the Name of Excellence*. New York: Oxford University Press.

United States Congress (1994). Goals 2000: Educate America Act.

United States Congress, Office of Technology Assessment (1993). *Adult literacy and new technologies: Tools for a lifetime*. Washington DC: US Government Printing Office.

Wiggenhorn, W. (1990). Motorola U: When training becomes an education. *Harvard Business Review*, July–August, 71–83.

Overview

Aims/Purpose

At the time this project was envisaged, workplace literacy bibliographies were sub-sections of larger bibliographies and literature reviews on literacy. Texts listed were more often 'how to' manuals for tutors than discussions of global issues. The aim of this literature review of workplace literacy is to provide some analysis of current issues through reference to the literature, and to help disseminate information, research and theory in a way that will enhance knowledge and practice. In particular, discussion and text references aim to highlight issues arising for the practice of literacy within recent organisational change, referred to in the literature as the 'New Work Order.'

The texts have been selected in an attempt to identify, organise and assess competing views and claims from different literatures and to redress possible imbalances. Contrasting models of literacy eg, functional and critical; banking and liberating; proper and improper; autonomous and ideological; and 'really useful knowledge' and 'fairly useful knowledge' are referenced.

Parameters

The scope of this literature review is restricted to issues impacting on literacy and paid workers in industrial countries, especially the UK, USA, Canada, Australia, and New Zealand. The review is also restricted by a wish to focus on *recent* changes in organisational theory and practice, to writings from 1980 to 1998 (ie, writings which deal with New Times and the New Work Order). There are, however, some important exceptions such as Paulo Freire's *Pedagogy of the Oppressed*, 1972, and Harry Braverman's *Labour and Monopoly Capital: The Degradation of Work in the Twentieth Century*, 1974. Freire's work was the precursor of a whole educational movement concerned with critical consciousness and politicisation, and Braverman looks at how the Marxist concept of alienation applies to work in the twentieth century.

The 1980s, with their New Right governments in Britain, the United States and elsewhere, have seen a a rapid and radical change in demands on education. In all countries included in this review, there has been an an upsurge in policy documents linking education to global competitiveness and industry texts which propose new directions in adult and workplace education policies.

Educators are having to take account of the acquisition of 'competencies' and how they affect progression in the workplace. In many instances, such radical and rapid upheavals have kept many writers in education and literacy focussed on pedagogical issues without being able to address wider political issues. In the UK, research has largely taken either a 'policy oriented' or 'social problem' approach. Brian Street notes 'a lack of pedagogic theory in adult education in general and of theory on adult literacy in particular' (Street, 1997:19) in the UK, observing the exception of Levine, 1982 and Jones and Charnley, 1978.

Perspectives

The literature seems to reflect three broad perspectives, although there is no clear division between them. Indeed, they often overlap, and authors may only partially agree with the ideas reflected in a particular view, or identify with aspects of more than one perspective:

1. *The functional view.*

Literacy is understood as a set of technical skills which can be measured, and in which people can be said to be competent or not yet competent. They are typically narrowly and functionally focussed, and linked with foundation level qualifications, or elementary schooling. Literacy is seen as the means by which organisations, and countries can improve their competitive edge. Poor literacy skills and schools are often blamed for a country's lack of global competitiveness. Job tasks and workers are assessed in a 'literacy audit', and providers aim to fill the 'skills gaps.'

2. *The liberal view.*

Literacy is seen to be broader than a set of necessary skills to perform a given task. The context of learning is taken into account, and workers are not blamed for their learning 'deficits'. Organisational communications systems, the attitudes of key personnel, and the level of democratic functioning in the workplace are all understood to impact on workers' literacies. Management, union/worker and educational interests are seen to be reconcilable. Workers are encouraged to make curriculum development contributions, and programmes are broadened to include special interests and literacy used in the community outside work.

3. *The radical/critical view.*

'Proper literacy' is literacy for active citizenship and necessarily has a political dimension. It is embedded in social and cultural practices and relations rather than being simply a technology. To be literate is to continually 'read' one's world (understand social, cultural, political aspects), to write and rewrite it, and thereby transform one's relationship to it. (Freire and Macedo,

1987). Management and worker interests are often significantly different, and sometimes irreconcilable.

The New Literacy studies
References will be drawn primarily from social science theory and in particular the 'New Literacy Studies'. This is a recent movement in which literacy is studied in the social, cultural, historical, political and economic practices of which they are a part, rather than primarily in psychological terms (see Barton, 1994; Gee 1997).

Management texts, research and reports, union and policy documents and guidelines are also included.

Audience

Intended readers are practitioners, policy makers, researchers, students, workplace trainers, trade union members and others interested in, or engaged in workplace literacy. It is hoped that the discussion of issues provided here will be clear to readers who are unfamiliar with the ideas addressed.

Format

The discussion begins by giving the background to the issues arising from the conjunction of literacy and the new work order. It outlines historical developments, changing organisational practices, beliefs about 'illiteracy', the current state of play, and the politics of literacy. The review is then divided into three parts.

Part One looks at themes and issues. These have been identified from a search of the literature. They are: *Crisis and competitiveness*; *High performance workplaces*; *The learning organisation*. Although this book deliberately sets out to look at the issues, rather than to review the 'how to' manuals, there are some important guidelines referenced, and an 'Implications for provision' section completes each theme.

The first theme, *Crisis and competitiveness*, discusses the literature concerned with international competition for markets, concomitant industry restructuring, and the way that literacy is linked as both a causal and a curative factor. It presents texts which offer an alternative reading of the situation.

The second theme, *High performance workplaces*, examines writings on some specific changes to organisations which have impacted on workers and their educational opportunities. These changes include a move to a focus on 'quality' organisations, the 'flexible' manipulations of workers, the impact of technology and reductions in the core workforce.

The third theme, *The learning organisation,* records a range of responses to the way that the New Work Order is seen to affect education, and vice versa. Various views on the educational value of the competency movement are offered as well as a discussion of how education transmits ideology. Claims about the doors that literacy can open for workers are examined.

At the end of the Background section and of each theme, references (which appear again in the full bibliography, Part Three) are listed under the following six categories:

> Social Science
> Management Texts
> Research/Reports
> Policy Documents
> Unions
> Practice/Guidelines

Part Two comprises annotations which are presented using the above categories. Each annotation is numbered. There are corresponding numbers on listings in the bibliography to facilitate cross-referencing. Not all references are annotated.

Part Three consists of an alphabetically-listed bibliography of all references which concludes the review. Only annotated references are coded.

Background

History

An analysis of the literature relating to literacy and the New Work Order needs to be placed within the history of the development of workers' literacies. An appropriate starting point would seem to be the industrial revolution in Britain and Europe. A number of social science theorists of the 'new literacy studies' provide thorough accounts.

Mary Hamilton traces historical roots in her account of literacy and adult education. She says:

> 'The history of the struggle for universal access to basic education has been tied up with the struggle for political enfranchisement, and in both of these adult education played a significant role.'
>
> (Hamilton, 1996: 143)

Colin Lankshear, with Moira Lawler, writes of developments and trends in literacy in the late eighteenth and early nineteenth centuries in the UK and how these were determined by one's social class:

> 'Within social life, the working class had a well-defined station to observe and maintain. Relations of deference, acceptance of authority, and willingness to be controlled by one's betters, were culturally enforced. These relations extended to education as well. Whether or not the poor received education, what they received, and under what conditions, were details that were largely outside the power of the working class to determine.' (Lankshear and Lawler, 1987:83)

He describes three worker initiatives during that period which impacted on literacy development for the working class: the Corresponding Societies of 1792–99, the struggle for a working class press, and the theory and practice of Chartist education. Lankshear discusses how a . . .

> ' . . .democratic and empowering form of literacy was constructed within the process of struggling for popular empowerment and a more democratic approach to government in Britain.' (ibid:85)

E.P.Thompson in *The Making of the English Working Class* traces the political, economic and cultural oppression of working people between 1790 and the 1830s, which resulted in the growth of working class consciousness whereby working people came to perceive their interests as workers as being distinct from those of other classes. (Thompson, 1963:213, 315)

Harvey Graff investigates three cities in Ontario, Canada, in the mid-nineteenth-century, to discover to what extent literacy functioned as an independent variable in bringing about social and material benefits for workers.

He finds that, as in Britain at the same time . . .

'literacy alone . . . that is, isolated from its moral basis – was feared as potentially subversive.' (Graff, 1986:23)

At this time, many politicians and writers in the UK identified impediments to what was regarded as a 'sound working class education', and sought to make cheap publications available to workers containing what was deemed 'really useful knowledge.'

Lankshear writes of how The Society for the Diffusion of Useful Knowledge (SDUK) was established in 1826, for the working class, but by middle class interests. He refers to *The Penny Magazine,* edited by Charles Knight, who stated the aims of the society were:

'to give the means of content to those who, for the most part, must necessarily remain in that station which requires great self-denial and great endurance.' (quoted from Simon, 1960, in Lankshear and Lawler, 1987:108)

Katherine Hughes examines the Society's work also, and explores the concept of 'really useful knowledge,' which, she says, 'underpinned many radical adult education initiatives in the 1970s and 1980s.' (Hughes, 1995:99). She compares these strategies with education in the UK in the 1990s, in which what she has called 'fairly useful knowledge,' is imparted. This latter, she says, embodies attempts to limit and control learning by means of competency based education, where knowledge is reduced to 'small pieces of credit . . . which limit tutor capacity to negotiate and respond to student interest.' (*ibid*:99)

Mary Hamilton comments on developments in the early twentieth century:

'Throughout this period there have been . . . worries about declining literacy standards. Rogers (1984) collected quotations from board of education reports from 1921, 1925, and 1939 which indicate concern from employers and educators alike that standards of basic literacy and numeracy were falling short of some notional but desirable level . . . . . These sources make fascinating reading because they are so similar to contemporary claims'

(Hamilton, 1996: 144)

Literacy crises are not new, maintains Graff (1986), but have surfaced at other times in history, particularly during times of large scale unheaval and rapid change. At such times concerns about a decline in literacy are voiced.

The changing nature of work

Much of the literature reviewed describes the evolution of work organisation from the turn of the century through to the post World War Two period in industrially developed countries, and from post war management to the management styles of the 1980s and 1990s in current 'free market' economies. Braverman's critique of modern work practices is briefly outlined below, as is the developing New Work Order of fast capitalism and 'high performance' workplaces.

Taylorism and Fordism

Around the early 1900s, industry began to be modelled on the innovations of Henry Ford, the car manufacturer who introduced the concept of mass production. Frederick Taylor then introduced his theory of scientific management, whereby companies were encouraged to focus on the most efficient use of time and energy for completing a task. Tasks were analysed and reassembled for efficiency and productivity, but tended to increase monotony and boredom. Laurie Field, in a handbook for trainers in Australia, explains:

> '*Taylor argued that the thinking and planning associated with work should be looked after by management, and that workers should be encouraged to do management's bidding by systems of incentives. Taylor's work practices are characterised by the fragmentation of jobs, the provision of individual incentives in such a way that cooperative group work is discouraged, and the removal of worker control over output.*' (Field, 1990:8)

Knowledge and control of work was held by managers, who conceived and designed products, while workers executed production. Informal communities of workers were replaced by a hierarchy of well paid, professional managers overseeing low paid, under-educated workers.

Frequently referred to in the literature as Taylorist or Fordist, these workplaces were characterised by mass production (for a commodities starved post World War Two population), and large workforces. During this period, however, trade unions were relatively strong. They were able to negotiate improved pay and conditions for workers. Jobs were usually for life. (see O'Connor 1994, Gowen 1996)

Industrialisation of the western world had turned a corner, but still reflected the values of old capitalism (eg. patriarchal responsibility for employees, exclusion of shop floor workers from planning and decision making). Work was alienating:

> '*Workers, hired from the neck down had only to follow directions and mechanically carry out a rather meaningless piece of a process they did not need to understand as a whole, and certainly did not control.*' (Gee et al, 1996:26)

Many management and educational texts concur in their opinion that these values and strategies are no longer economically effective, if, indeed, they ever were. (compare, for instance, Darville, 1992; Forrester et al, 1995; Senge, 1990; Thompson and McHugh, 1990).

A Marxist view

In 1974, Harry Braverman published a seminal critique of twentieth century work practices: *Labor and Monopoly Capital: The Degradation of Work in the Twentieth Century* Braverman examines the impact of technology and the organisation of capitalist production on workers. His central argument is that new technologies result in the deskilling of jobs, allowing management greater control, and degrading work for the majority of the employed population. (Braverman, 1974)

Some writers argue that Braverman's writings are no longer relevant because workplaces are no longer organised in the way he describes, while others see that the changes and lack of worker control of which he warns have simply accelerated under the guise of a new cooperation between management and workers. Laurie Field comments:

> 'It has become increasingly obvious that Taylorist work practices are not an appropriate basis for the organisation of work and workers in Australia. A goal that has been attracting a lot of attention recently is the development of more cooperative, participative relations between workers and management . . . . . The achievement of such a goal requires changes in job design, management structures and systems, and labour-management relations.' (Field, 1990:19)

Gee, referring to Gramsci's theories (1971), describes this as the new hegemony:

> ' . . . In modern developed capitalistic societies the use of overt force and control is ot necessary because non-elites unwittingly (though partially and often with resistance) internalise a set of beliefs and values that actually represent not their own interests, but those of elites.' (Gee, 1994b:14)

A New Work Order

Under the 'new capitalism' or 'fast capitalism' of the 1980s, changes in workplace organisation have become more rapid. Many question the democracy of the new order, and note that the worker's mind, as well as her/his body are now essential to the production process:

> 'The emphasis now is on the (active) knowledge and flexible learning needed to design, market, perfect and vary goods and services as symbols of identity, not on the actual product itself as a material good.' (Gee et al, 1996:26. See, also, Agger, 1989)

In their book *The New Work Order*, Jim Gee, Glynda Hull and Colin Lankshear explore how workers are asked to invest their hearts, minds and bodies fully in their work. But they also make an important point about the extent to which the fast capitalist order is a reality:

> *'When we refer here to the new capitalism, we are specifically making reference to the thus far unevenly realised worldview contained in a large number of quasi-popular business texts.' (Gee et al, 1996:16)*

Gee is elsewhere more specific about the intent of 'popular' business texts:

> *'They seek not just to describe but to create a 'new reality'. Theirs is a world in which the boundaries between what 'is' , what 'will be', what 'must be' and 'what ought to be' is frequently blurred.' (Gee, 1994a:2)*

Many workers are already experiencing this reality. As organisations rush to capture this vision, features of the New Work Order seem eerily close. Writing in 1992, the authors of 'Workplace 2000', put their view of current and predicted changes this way:

> *'Working will be more of an economic exchange. Regardless of where someone works, he or she will be expected to 'sign up', 'join up' and 'buy into' the corporate vision . . . . . each American will have to decide on the value of that exchange.' (Boyett and Conn, 1992: 114, 115)*

Training for High Performance

Workplace education and training have played a key role in the New Work Order. Companies have reduced the size of their workforces and sought to upgrade and multiply the skills of their existing workforce to fill gaps, and to increase commitment. A University of Leeds research report found:

> *'Many firms were making employees redundant, but at the same time they were expecting more of those who remained.' (Payne, 1993b: 24)*

Training budgets are now commonplace in modern workplaces, although allocations are not even. Hensley quotes a 1989 report by the Commission on Workforce Quality and Labor Market Efficiency which notes that only 14% of training budgets were allocated to production and assembly workers in 1988 in the US. Whereas:

> *'..a vast majority of employer investment was made in higher wage clerical, sales, marketing or management employees.' (Hensley, 1993: 3)*

The 'problem of illiteracy'

The literature traces the emergence of a more explicitly ideological approach to the literacy of adults focussing on those in productive sectors. Important contributions to this discussion can be found in *Literacies of Power* (Macedo, 1996) and in *Education Under Siege* (Aronowitz and Giroux,1985)

UNESCO

In 1942, US army recruits who had not progressed beyond grade 9 were defined as illiterates, kindling the current crisis mentality. From the late 1960s, the 'economic push for literacy' (Darville 1992) emerged.

UNESCO reports on international literacy deficits, made links between literacy and economic competitiveness:

> *'If developing countries could not afford to educate all their adults, they should focus on those adults working in the productive sectors; to provide literacy instruction would make them even better workers.' (UNESCO 1976)*

Governments and UNESCO urged that programmes be put in place to bring populations to functional literacy, as measured by a certain number of years in school. (Drouin 1990)

This 'awakening' to the 'problem of illiteracy' began to appear in other Non-Government Organisation reports, education and management prescriptions.

International Literacy Year, 1990

In the 1980s, literacy became firmly established as the path to economic growth in the literature of industrial management, governments, and of many educators and literacy workers. (Ooijens, 1994) It was even considered 'indispensable to rapid socio-economic development'. (Oxenham, 1980:17)

By International Literacy Year, some countries had conducted national studies to determine the functional literacy of the population. In Canada, the UK and Australia, numbers of adults who were 'functionally illiterate' or had serious literacy difficulties, were estimated at between roughly 10% and 25% in various nations, depending on how measurements were made and boudaries drawn. (Compare Wickert, 1989; Montigny, 199; Hamilton, 1987.)

The politics of schooling

Harry Braverman, in *Labor and Monopoly Capital*, shows how skill, which is the ability to do something well [craft mastery], has come to be equated with years of schooling. He reminds us of the historical and current agenda for the push for literacy:

> *'The ability to read, write, and perform simple arithmetical operations is demanded by the urban environment, not just in jobs but also for consumption, for conformity to the rules of society and obedience to the law. Reading and figuring are, apart from all their other meanings, the elementary attributes of a manageable population . . .' (Braverman, 1974:436)*

He describes how (a) the enlarged school system has been used to reduce unemployment figures and (b) years of schooling and educational qualifications

have been used by employers in recruiting staff, not because of the job requirements, but as an easy means of screening applicants. (*ibid*:348–440) Where the
'illiterate' have been consulted it has been reported that other barriers to quality
of life are a more pressing concern:

> '*literacy is seldom a first priority among those who are themselves unlettered.
> When given an opportunity to define their own needs, they are likely to stress
> first their economic problems, followed by such personal concerns as family living,
> child care, health and nutrition.*' (Hunter and Harman, 1979)

Literacy in the context of the workplace

Alongside the call for higher literacy standards both in first and third world
countries, came a gradual saturation of markets. The 1970s saw world reces-
sions and dumping of products, the beginnings of large scale cuts in the
workforce and of lengthy workers' strikes. The literature records a move to a
new management style arising out of a crisis in industrial management and an
attack on schools by industry, who have themselves utilised the language of
education for their own purposes. Each of these factors is described below.

The Japanese

By the early 1980s organisational management in the western world began to
be influenced by Japanese practice, where the focus was on product quality
and worker identification with the goals of management. Governments and
industry have adopted these practices in order to increase and maintain global
competitiveness. The Total Quality movement, as promoted by Deming and
'Workplace 2000', where [it is predicted] hierarchy will be replaced by shared
goals and company loyalty, have been the lynch pins around which the New
Work Order has developed. (Compare Deming 1986, Boyett and Conn 1992,
O'Connor 1994, Thompson and McHugh, 1990.)

Co-opting the language of education

The language of education had begun to enter the workplace, but with a
difference of meaning. Critical theorists, in particular social linguist Jim Gee,
observe the recent trend of 'co-opting' of words which are frequently used in
education to create in workers a sense of personal power and control over
their working lives and learning, words like 'liberation', 'empowerment',
'trust', 'vision' and 'self directed learning' (Gee *et al*, 1996:29)

The failings of schools

Changing work structures, quality assurance practices, increased technology,
diversification for niche markets, all demand more literacy skills of otherwise
skilled workers. By the year 2000, claim Boyett and Conn:

'There will be no place for the functionally illiterate. In fact, there may be no place for anyone without at least some level of college education.' (Boyett and Conn 1992:276)

Schools, it is claimed, are inadequate to meet the changed demands of industry, and too many workers are ill equipped to handle even the most rudimentary literacy tasks. (Drucker 1993)

Katherine Hughes (1995) is concerned at such scapegoating of education to account for an underclass created by an uncompetitive British economy:

'The declining economy is blamed on a failure of morality caused by the laxness of teachers and parents and a dependency culture, whilst the 'poor law' is tightened most punitively.' (Hughes, 1995:100)

Sheila Collins, in her article *Workplace Literacy: Corporate Tool or Worker Empowerment*, is sceptical of the motives of business in criticising the performance of schools, and asks:

'Is business's new concern for education the chance it has long awaited to wrest control from professional educators over socialisation of the values and attitudes necessary to maintain labour peace in a period of greater economic instability?' (Collins, 1989: 27)

Aronowitz and Giroux have no doubts about this, and query current basic assumptions about the aim of education:

'. . . . instrumental rationality underlies most academic and vocational counselling; the doctrine of 'career and occupational' education has progressively made deep incursions into the liberal arts orientation of school authorities. The proliferation of 'career days' at the junior high as well as the high school levels is all too common. It signifies the triumph of the school-business partnership approach to learning motivation.' (Aronowitz and Giroux, 1985:192)

Union influence

In all these developments, trade unions have gradually come to have less and less influence on traditional workplace issues. Now training, as much as pay and conditions, is a key bargaining issue. While the involvement and endorsement of workplace training and education is considered vital by many practitioners, concerns are expressed that unions' sanctioning of the New Work Order stifles critical debate. (Brown, 1994)

Jane Mace notes that although trade union education *has* been a key area for bargaining, basic skills education in the workplace came late as a union issue, travelling, in the UK, on a separate line from the 1970s campaign for a 'right to read'. (Mace, 1987:79–94)

References
Social Science Theory

Agger, B. (1989). *Fast Capitalism: A Critical Theory of Significance*. Urbana: University of Illinois.

Aronowitz, S. and Giroux, H. (1985). *Education Under Siege: The Conservative, Liberal and Radical Debate over Schooling*. South Hadley, Massachusetts: Bergin and Garvey.

Barton, D. (1994). *Literacy: An Introduction to the Ecology of Written Language*. Oxford: Blackwell.

Braverman, H. (1974). *Labour and Monopoly Capital: The Degradation of Work in the Twentieth Century*. London, New York: Monthly Review Press.

Brown, M. (1994). *Literacies and the Workplace*. Geelong, Victoria: Deakin University.

Collins, S. (1989). Workplace Literacy: Corporate Tool or Worker Empowerment? *Social Policy*, 20 (1) Summer. New York: City University.

Darville, R. (1992). The Economic Push for Literacy: Expansive or Restrictive? In *Proceedings of Adult Literacy: An International Urban Perspective.* New York: UNESCO

Drucker, P. F. (1993). *Post-Capitalist Society* . New York: Harper.

Field, L. (1990). *Skilling Australia*. Melbourne: Longman Cheshire.

Forrester, K., Payne, J., and Ward, K. (1995). *Workplace Learning* Aldershot: Avebury. Ashgate Publishing Ltd.

Freire, P. (1972). *Pedagogy of the Oppressed* . Harmondsworth: Penguin.

Freire, P. and Macedo, D. (1987). *Reading the Word and the World* . London: Routledge and Kegan Paul Ltd.

Gee, J. P. (1994a). *New Alignments and Old Literacies: From Fast Capitalism to the Canon*. Carlton: Australian Reading Association.

Gee, J.P (1994b). Quality, Science and the Lifeworld. *Critical Forum*. 3 (1). Leichhardt: ALBSAC.

Gee, J.P. (1997). *The New Literacy Studies: A Retrospective View.* 'Situated Literacies' Conference paper, Lancaster University.

Gee, J. P., Hull, G. and Lankshear, C. (1996). *The New Work Order* St. Leonards: Allen and Unwin.

Gowen, S. G. (1996). How the Reorganisation of Work Destroys Everyday Knowledge. In Hautecoeur, J.P. Ed. *Basic Education and Work: Alpha 96*. Toronto: UNESCO and Culture Concepts

Graff, H. (1986). *The Legacies of Literacy: Continuities and Contradictions in Western Culture and Society* Bloomington: Indiana University Press.

Hamilton, M. (1996) Adult Literacy and Basic Education. In Fieldhouse, R, Ed. *A History of Modern British Education* Leicester, NIACE

Hughes, K. (1995). Really Useful Knowledge. In Mayo, M., and Thompson, J., Eds. *Adult Learning, Critical Intelligence and Social Change*. Leicester: NIACE.

Jones, H.A. and Charnley, A.H. (1978). *Adult Literacy − A Study of its Impact*. Leicester: NIACE.

Lankshear, C. and Lawler, M. (1987). *Literacy, Schooling and Revolution* . London: Falmer Press.

Levine, K. (1982). *Functional Literacy: Fond Illusions and False Economies*. Harvard Educational Review, 52(3)

Mace, J. (1987) Adult Literacy: Campaigns and Movements. In Mace, J. and Yarnit, M. (1987) *Time Off to Learn: Paid Education Leave and Low Paid Workers*. London: Methuen.

Macedo, D. (1996) Literacies of Power: What Americans are Not Allowed to Know. *Journal of Negro Education*. Vol 65 (2)

O'Connor, P. (1994). Ed. *Thinking Work*. Sydney: ALBSAC

Ooijens, J. (1994). *Literacy for Work Programs*. Amsterdam: John Benjamins Publishing Co.

Oxenham, J. (1980). *Literacy: Writing, Reading and Social Organisation*. London: Routledge and Kegan Paul.

Rogers, B. (1984) The Trend of Reading Standards Reassessed. *Educational Research*. 26 (3.)

Simon, B. (1960) *Studies in the History of Education 1780 – 1870*. London: Lawrence and Wishart.

Street, B. (1984). *Literacy in Theory and Practice*. Cambridge: Cambridge University Press.

Street, B. (1997). *Adult Literacy in the United Kingdom: A History of Research and Practice*. Lancaster: Research and Practice in Adult Literacy (RAPAL).

Thompson, E. P. (1963). *The Making of the English Working Class*. Harmondsworth: Penguin.

Thompson, P. and McHugh, D. (1990). *Work Organisations*. London: The MacMillan Press Ltd.

Management Texts

Boyett, J. H. and Conn, H. P. (1992). *Workplace 2000: The Revolution Reshaping American Business*. New York: Plume Penguin.

Deming, W. E. (1986). *Out of the Crisis*. Cambridge, Mass: MIT Center for Advanced Engineering Study.

Drucker, P. F. (1993). *Post-Capitalist Society*. New York: Harper.

Senge, P. (1990). *The Fifth Discipline: The Art and Practice of the Learning Organisation*. New York: Doubleday.

Policy

Drouin, M. J. (1990). *Workforce Literacy: An Economic Challenge for Canada* . Montreal: Hudson Institute.

Reports

Hunter, C. and Harman, D. (1979). *Adult Literacy in the United States: A Report to the Ford Foundation* . New York: McGraw Hill.

Montigny, G. (1991). *Adult Literacy in Canada: Results of a National Study*. Ottawa: Statistics Canada.

Payne, J. (1993b). Learning at Work. Final Report of the Leeds Adult Learners at Work Project. Leeds: Department of Adult Continuing Education, University of Leeds.

Payne, J., Forrester, K. and Ward, K. (1993). *Adult Learners at Work: Perspectives on Training and Education at Work*. Leeds: University of Leeds.

UNESCO. (1976). *The Experimental World Literacy Programme: A Critical Assessment*. Paris: UNESCO Press.

Wickert, R. (1989). *No Single Measure: A Survey of Australian Adult Literacy*. Sydney: Institute of Technical and Adult Teacher Education, Sydney College of Advanced Education.

Unions

Hensley, S. (1993) Union Roles in Workplace Literacy. *Catalyst*. 3 (23)

PART ONE
CURRENT THEMES AND ISSUES

Crisis and competitiveness

Global restructuring

Any discussion of the literature relating to workplace literacy must begin by looking at the global economic context in which this endeavour occurs. This chapter highlights some of the key attitudes of the new workplace, considered necessary by supporters of fast capitalism. These include attitudes towards labour and markets, including a focus on profit making, which require workers to 'buy into' company goals and develop and sell their knowledge in an entreprenerial fashion. These attitudes, by the parameters they set, shape practice in workplace education.

Labour and markets

Since the 1960s, the West increasingly faced competition from emerging industrial economies such as Japan, Korea and China, who could produce more cheaply because of a vast, cheap labour pool. Over the past decade or more, according to the management literature, this saturation of global markets with mass produced goods has required business enterprise to diversify its product range, to decrease its labour intensity [sack a lot of people], and to concentrate on quality, custom made goods for a selected [or created] market:

> 'Mass production, large work forces and low prices are being replaced by rationalised workplaces with sophisticated technology, producing quality goods for niche markets.' (Wiggenhorn, 1990:72)

In order to reduce production costs, companies are looking to cheaper labour markets. Factories have been set up in countries where labour is cheap, and this has contributed to a decline in the number of jobs at home, particularly in the manufacturing sector. Writing about the 'coming irrelevance of corporate nationality', Robert Reich shows:

> 'By the last decade of the century, however, global competition had altered the tacit rules of American capitalism . . . . (it) was now organised relentlessly around profits, not patriotism. When profitability requires that production be shifted from an American factory to a foreign one, the American executive hesitates not.' (Reich, 1992:140)

He adds:

> 'National corporations are turning into global webs whose high volume, standardised activities are undertaken wherever labor is cheapest worldwide.' (ibid: 304)

Commenting on the emergence of this trend, Aronowitz and DiFazio offer specific examples:

> 'Global capitalism, still largely US based, in which national boundaries were no longer (if they ever were) sacrosanct, produced a parallel industrial regime, the global assembly line . . . An 'American-made' automobile is likely to contain a Japanese fuel pump, a Mexican-made exhaust system, and Malaysian-produced windshield wipers – or to have been assembled in Japan, Mexico or Korea.' (Aronowitz and Di Fazio, 1994:83–84)

Moreover, they contend that because it was cheaper to import raw materials than to process them in the US, employment in related industries was drastically reduced and in some cases, the industries closed down for domestic production. (ibid: 84) Although these are not new trends, communications and production technologies have enabled this to occur on a greater scale than in earlier times. Accordingly, trade union power has been undercut. (See Cornfield, 1987.) In the West, the decline in manufacturing, the rise in the use of technology, and the need to find new and diverse markets are reasons given for a burgeoning of the service industry. (See Johnson and Packer 1987.)

Lean and mean organisations

The New Work Order is now focussed, as Reich states, 'relentlessly around profits.' This applies not only to private sector organisations but has had a shattering effect on the public sector also, in that public welfare is no longer the *modus operandi*. Hospitals, schools and tertiary institutions, once mandated to provide the best possible health and education services to their communities, today increasingly only do so if the user pays. Jane Mace comments:

> 'Organisations once designed to provide education and health are now selling modules and packages . . . . The 'Gaffer's angle' is in the way.' (Mace, 1992a:12)

Engendering commitment to corporate goals

Corporate leaders noticed the loyalty to the company which was achievable in some countries, especially Japan. Training of the workforce was identified as a key factor in gaining worker commitment to corporate goals, [sharing the vision], participating maximally in production or corporate decisions, and increasing and sharing their knowledge for the benefit of the company. Reich observes:

'The Japanese . . . have been spending about $1000 more on training each American worker then is spent by American employers in the same country.' (Reich, 1992:147)

With a combination of shared vision and 'knowledge', the worker, at any level of the workforce, would then 'have the courage' to do the work that was once the responsibility of management: to try new ways of thinking and acting, to take risks and to experiment. She or he would have the courage to utilise high level problem solving and communication skills with individuals and in teams in order to increase profits for the organisation.

The knowledge worker

This term, used increasingly in management texts, is explained and discussed by critical theorists, notably James Paul Gee.

'The business world, as part and parcel of massive global economic, technological, and social change, now sees 'knowledge' as its primary value. Contemporary, globally competitive businesses don't any longer really compete on the basis of their products or services per se. They compete, rather, on the basis of how much learning and knowledge they can use as leverage in order to expeditiously invent, produce, distribute and market their goods and services, as well as to innovatively vary and customise them.' (Gee et al, 1996:5)

In discussing the benefits, as he sees them, of the 'employee society' (of knowledge workers), Drucker claims:

'Knowledge workers . . . own the 'means of production', that is, their knowledge. And knowledge workers account for almost a third of the total workforce of a developed country.' (Drucker, 1993:64)

However, that 'means of production' must be sold to the employer, and, acutely so today, it's a buyer's market. Drouin agrees with Drucker's assertions about the importance of 'knowledge work',

'The real post industrial revolution is not a service revolution, but a cerebral one in which value is produced less by skilled hands than by skilled minds.' (Drouin, 1990:52)

Unions see the possibility of workers having some voice, and work with industry to encourage their participation. Cornfield argues that western industrial countries have learned from the Japanese experience that limited worker involvement in decision making may increase productivity, quality and labour peace (Cornfield, 1987). The definition of literacy, while still passive and functional, comes to include not only reading and writing, but also 'learning to learn', listening, creative thinking and problem solving, motivation, interpersonal skills, organisational effectiveness and other 'skills' which allow workers to be 'self managing' (Carnevale *et al*,

1990). Literacy development, in these terms, becomes a tool for creating company-committed workers:

> *'The knowledge-based organisation therefore requires that everyone take responsibility for that organisation's objectives, contribution, and, indeed, for its behaviour as well.' (Drucker, 1993:108)*

The value of workplace education and training, to nations seeking to have a competitive edge in the shrinking global market place, has risen.

The literacy crisis

Texts presented in this chapter illustrate attitudes to the so-called literacy crisis, which is actually a crisis for industry in a shrinking global marketplace. Education and training are linked to productivity and profits by government policy as well as industrial interests.

The increasing crisis of global competition for markets has turned the attention of business and governments towards the quality of education. Lack of literacy is at fault. Aronowitz and Giroux quote American government papers:

> *'In the words of the National Commission on Excellence in Education, we are a 'nation at risk' . . . the Carnegie Foundation report argues that 'the teaching profession is in crisis in this country' and the National Task Force on Education for Economic Growth claims that 'a real emergency is upon us.'' (Aronowitz and Giroux, 1985:199)*

Industry and Governments cite concern about economic performance internationally, in commissioned reports. One such in the USA was *A Nation at Risk*, which stated:

> *'If an unfriendly power had attempted to impose on America the mediocre educational performance that exists today, we might have viewed it as an act of war.' (quoted in Boyett and Conn, 1992:267)*

Aronowitz and Giroux are concerned at the relationship being drawn . . .

> *'between the state of the U.S. economy, with its lagging domestic performance and its shrinking preeminence in the international marketplace, and the failure of the schools to educate students to meet the economic needs of the dominant society.' (ibid:199)*

The role of education and training

The aim of education, articulated in management texts and in supporting government policy documents, should be to increase a country's competitive edge on the international market. The Australian Education and Training policy states:

'*Education and Training are pivotal to economic growth, international competitiveness, increased productivity, the mobility of the population and to the level and standard of living.*' (*Australian Chamber of Manufacturers*, 1991:8–13)

and . . .

'*There is now, one can pretty confidently say, widespread recognition that a major upgrading of our performance in education is crucial to arresting our relative economic decline . . .*' (*ibid*:8–13)

Linking literacy to productivity

There is now a widespread body of literature from industrialised nations to support the view that significant basic skills deficits exist in these countries, and that education and training will increase economic productivity. (compare BCEL, 1988; Department of Trade and Industry, 1994; Drouin, 1990; Keating, 1994) In her introduction to a US Department of Education publication, Ann McLaughlin, secretary for the US Department of Labor maintains:

'*. . . [In the approaching new century] . . . Employers will place a premium on higher levels of reading computation, communication and reasoning skills. Such skills will be vital to our domestic economic growth, as well as our ability to compete abroad.*' (*Harman and Lerche, 1988: introd.*)

She adds:

'*Improving basic skills in the workplace is yet another way that the private sector can ensure that the United States remains competitive in the world economy.*' (*ibid*)

In the UK, a government White Paper echoes these proclamations:

'*Hard working people with high skills, and the knowledge and understanding to use them to the full, are the lifeblood of a modern, internationally competitive economy . . . A fulfilled workforce meeting individual targets . . . will be a world class workforce.*' (*Department of Trade and Industry*, 1994:30)

In a commissioned survey of employer responses in the US it is claimed:

'*. . . the root cause of many different problems related to employment, productivity, increased costs turnover and even injury are, in fact, a function of an inadequate level of literacy.*' (*The Omega Group* 1989:5)

William Wiggenhorn, writing about the Motorola U training and education programme in the Harvard Business Review, remarked:

'*. . . documenting [our] installations one by one, we concluded that about half of our 25,000 manufacturing and support people in the United States failed to* *meet the seventh grade yardstick in English and math.' (Wiggenhorn, 1990: 78)*

Government and business reports cite the costs to business of inadequate literacy skills. A US Business Council for Effective Literacy leaflet, *Functional Literacy Hurts Business*, tells employers:

> *'Millions of employees suffering from various degrees of illiteracy are costing their companies daily through low productivity, workplace accidents and supervisory time.' (BCEL, 1988)*

Barriers to employment, even social ills, are attributed to perceived worker deficits:

> *'More and more, American employers will no longer enjoy the luxury of selecting from a field of workers with strong basic skills. The demand for labor will create opportunities for those who are less skilled: the disadvantaged will move up the labor queue and be hired in spite of obvious skill deficiencies' (Carnevale et al, 1990:5)*

Further:

> *'Deficiency in basic skills stands as the final barrier to employment of the poor and disadvantaged . . . Such skill deficiencies are also among the principal causes of the social pathology that torments the poor.' (ibid:14)*

Responding to the crisis

The general response by many academics, providers of workplace education as well as business and government, is that the literacy crisis is real. Implicit in this acceptance is the view that the goal of education is to make companies and countries more competitive. The common solution has been to promote basic skills training to raise basic skills levels of current and future workers in the best interests of workers, management, and the country.

Government and industry

Slogans have been created by governments to sell lifelong education and training to the public and to industry: 'Clever country' [Australia], 'Surpassing ourselves' [USA] (O'Connor, 1994:6) and 'Skill New Zealand' (Education and Training Support Agency, 1993).

In the UK the Confederation of British Industry encourages National Training Targets to be met through 'Investors in People.' (CBI, 1989) At the same time policies reflect governments' reluctance to take an active lead, indeed a willingness to allow industry to determine the direction of training reform. The USA report, *Workplace Basics: The Skills Employers Want*, reflects a similar perspective:

'Employers are beginning to see that they must assist their current and future workers to achieve competency in workplace basics if they are to become competitive.' and 'A workforce with sound basic skills will strengthen its employer's ability to compete.' (Carnevale et al, 1990:1)

A report for US government, *The Bottom Line*, urges the strengthening of employee basic skills to benefit a company's overall performance. (Harman and Lerche, 1988) The Business Council for Effective Literacy in New York, in its brief pamphlet entitled *The Connection between Employee Basic Skills and Productivity*, reports that there is a definite connection between employee basic skills programmes and increased productivity. They illustrate the point with specific examples of companies reporting decreased costs and increased productivity after basic skills provision. (BCEL, 1993:1–4)

Basic skills education providers

Basic skills education providers, however aware of the narrowness of government and industry interpretations, market their services accordingly. In the executive summary of the Adult Reading and Learning Association's Workbase [NZ] national report on *Literacy at Work*, Liz Moore states:

'The pursuit of increased competitiveness by governments and industry is really only possible if those members of the workforce who are needed to bring about the workplace of New Zealand's future get access to new training opportunities.' (Moore and Benseman, 1993:10)

The Basic Skills Agency (formerly ALBSU), established in the UK to promote and assist the development of basic skills in the community and the workplace, asserts the positive economic effects of literacy programmes in its promotional publications:

'It is widely recognised that the lack of an adequately trained workforce is a major factor inhibiting the competitiveness of British Industry.' (ALBSU, 1995:8)

Rosie Wickert draws the following implications from her Australian literacy survey:

'A successful economy needs the solid base of a literate and numerate workforce . . . it's about re-training . . . Employers and unions alike recognise this.' (Wickert, 1989:39)

Refuting the crisis

Critics question a number of assumptions, including the strength of the links between education and productivity and between lack of literacy and years of schooling. They claim workers are being unfairly blamed for failings in economic and industrial management, and that many of these workers perceive the situation clearly and resist management attempts to 'educate'. Finally, they ask whether education should, in fact, serve the economic ends of a few.

Questioning the links

Glynda Hull argues that solutions posed by industry and many basic skills providers are too simple. In her ethnographic study of people's experience of a vocational education programme and subsequent work, Hull remarks on the way policy documents decry the low level of literacy in the population:

> 'The problem is much more complicated than a deficit in skills, and its solution much more difficult than devising a new skills building program or providing workplace literacy instruction.' (Hull, 1991a:61)

She explores how people experienced a vocational education programme in Banking, and the relationship between that programme, the jobs they train for, and literacy and the current crisis rhetoric. Hull discovered that the skills needs stressed on the programme, i.e. interpersonal skills and literacy, didn't match those needed on the job. The work in fact:

> 'required little knowledge of banking and few social skills – in direct contrast to the emphasis in the program – nor did they require much reading or any writing, which runs counter to the basic skills literature and the widespread claims that . . . industries are suffering because workers lack advanced literacy skills and high-tech competencies.' (ibid:60)

Forrester, Payne and Ward (1995) and Luke (1992:3–15) also critically analyse the rhetoric that education and training are panaceas for an economic crisis. They assert little causal relationship between education and training and economic performance. Murray Saunders, in his paper *The Integrative Principle: Higher Education and Work-Based Learning*, adds:

> 'While processes embedded in initiatives like work based learning might help to create a 'learning culture' in an organisation, the contribution that such a culture might make to international competitiveness is still uncertain and remains a hope rather than a substantiated likely outcome.' (Saunders, 1995a:211)

In the US, Hanna Fingeret expresses her concern:

> ' . . . We hear talk of literacy as a way of keeping your present job, protecting yourself from obsolescence, and supporting America's present position of competitiveness in the global market place.' (Fingeret, 1988:5)

She is uncomfortable with

> 'the workplace literacy thrust . . . the concern that economics is becoming the only legitimate rationale for literacy work.' (ibid:6)

Flawed figures

In Canada, Marie-Jose Drouin examines some functional literacy test statistics, and recognises that some assessments are methodologically flawed because functional literacy skills are equated with a certain level of school attainment (e.g. grade 8–9). Still these measures are used to support claims about an illiterate workforce:

> '25 million American workers need to improve their basic skills . . . A survey taken in 1987 by Southam Inc. indicates that approximately 4.5 million adult Canadians have inadequate or insufficient literacy skills.' (Drouin, 1990:22–23)

No magic elixirs

Peter O'Connor explores the 'economically competitive' argument and the effect of International Literacy Year, 1990, in accelerating the process. In his introduction to *Thinking Work* Volume One, he warns of promising the impossible:

> 'To view or promote workplace education as the saviour of economic, industrial and personal problems can lead to unrealistic expectations and accompanying dangers. It is misleading to suggest that shortfalls in basic skills are responsible for lower productivity levels, the majority of industrial accidents, poor product quality or wastage, or missed employment opportunities.' (O'Connor, 1994:30)

However, he concedes:

> ' . . . basic skills upgrading may have a modest but significant role to play in alleviating some of these problems' (ibid:30)

Masking a deeper crisis

O'Connor addresses educators in this admonishment:

> ' playing to the fears of foreign capitalism, national debt, the growth of an alienated 'underclass', declining wages and living standards for workers, and in the absence of any organised resistance, business has been able to largely manipulate and dictate the terms of the debate, while often presenting itself in the guise of 'innocent bystanders'. The education sector has been conspicuously silent and timid in its contributions and critiques.' (O'Connor, 1994: 5)

Sheryl Gowen suggests the highlighting of the 'crisis' is a cynical action on the part of governments:

> 'The national movement to declare a state of crisis in levels of adult literacy, and the back to basics movement serve to deflect attention away from conditions of poverty and marginalisation that give rise not only to illiteracy but also to poor health care, inadequate housing, and artificial job ceilings, all realities in the lives of far too many men, women, and children in this country.' (Gowen, 1992)

Writing about *How the Reorganisation of Work Destroys Everyday Knowledge*, Gowen says:

> 'It is not coincidental that the 'literacy crisis' has occurred in tandem with the reorganisation of the workplace.' (Gowen, 1996: 12)

Glynda Hull adds that there is too much faith in the power of literacy and too little credence in people's abilities. She states:

> ' . . . the popular discourse. . tends to . . . devalue . . . and mis-characterise literacy as a curative for problems that literacy alone cannot solve . . . and that this . . . obscure[s] other social and economic problems.' (Hull 1994:47)

Peter Freebody and Anthony Welch, writing about the current literacy debates in Australia, claim that arguments for a crisis deflect attention away from the productive directions of reevaluation and reform, and allow for domestication of the curriculum. They label the discourse of crisis a 'confection' and ask whose crisis it really is, and who benefits from the proposed solutions. (Freebody and Welch, 1993) A European report adds:

> 'Human resources, including education and training, is only one factor among ten that affect a country's international competitiveness.' (World Economic Forum 1989)

Illiteracy or alienation?

Sheryl Gowen, in her book *The Politics of Workplace Literacy*, suggests that apparent 'functional illiteracy' may be more a consequence of resistance on the part of alienated workers. She maintains that issues in the workplace distort the picture, that workers well able to engage in literacy practices outside the workplace, resist the particular forms of literacy imposed on them, and the skills they have go unrecognised. She outlines the way researchers, policy makers and others recognise the impact that restructured workplaces and technology have had on what counts as literacy, and yet the literature commonly refers to the skills deficit of the individual (Gowen, 1992). Gowen reports that management believed workers could not deal with written communication, and explains:

> 'This rendered invisible, the employees' beliefs about text and knowledge and the strategies they use to acquire and share information' (ibid, 1992)

Questioning basic assumptions

James Turk places the 'crisis' in its sociopolitical context:

> 'Limited literacy is not a major cause of unemployment – lack of jobs is. Limited literacy is not a major cause of accidents and disease at work – unsafe working

conditions and widespread use of toxic substances are . . . Limited literacy is not a principal cause of low productivity – inadequate capital investment, outdated technology, poor work organisation are.' (Turk 1990:269)

The rightness of a marriage between education and the business community, indeed between education and national economic performance, is seldom questioned, even within schools. Aronowitz and Giroux, writing about 'the crisis in public philosophy', argue against pervading assumptions. They maintain that in the current model of economic rationality,

> ' . . . *public education is defined primarily through a struggle for economic success and individual mobility . . . (which) suggests that economics are more important to our nation and schools than our commitment to democratic principles . . . The new philosophy is tied largely to assumptions that view schools as means to increasing individual achievement and promoting industrial needs. Such a view makes it difficult to defend public education in political and ethical terms.' (Aronowitz and Giroux, 1985:203, 204)*

Gee, examining the convergence between cognitive science and fast capitalism, notes:

> ' . . . *the language and viewpoints here have worn so smooth so quickly that we may not stop to think that the goals of school reformers could have been different from and, at various points contesting with, the goals of fast capitalism or any other market scheme.' (Gee, 1994a:11)*

Giroux and Aronowitz conclude:

> *'Learning is a way to power and gratification, but neo-conservatives have no program for empowerment, only for providing human capital able to make American business viable once more in the world market.' (Aronowitz and Giroux, 1985:215)*

Some implications for provision

The literature surveyed in this section warns of the difficulties in negotiating and delivering education in the current global economic climate. It also indicates a need for providers to approach workplace literacy with an awareness of widely different claims arising from different ideological positions. Compare, for instance:

> *'If the current demographic and economic trends continue, American business will have to hire a million new workers a year who can't read, write, or count.' (David Kearns, chairman of Xerox, quoted in Boyett and Conn, 1992:267)*

and

' . . .for the most part, this is a misplaced emphasis, a slogan that is oriented to promoting fear and anxiety so that a new wave of school policy may be accepted. Most Janeys and Johnnys can follow written orders, read newspapers and make calculations in hundreds of thousands of jobs.' (Aronowitz and Giroux, 1985:64)

Low literacy levels

A relationship can be seen between the outcry about low literacy levels and current drives to 'rationalise' workplaces by increasing technology, decreasing workforces and multiskilling. Is there a real crisis, or an increased demand created by organisational restructuring and technological advances? Are new literacy skills actually required for the job? Providers adopting crisis rhetoric in pursuing contracts may unwittingly support changes which damage the interests of low paid and vulnerable workers.

Theorists, researchers and providers will need to debate the intentions of slogans such as 'Skill New Zealand', 'Clever Country' and 'Lifelong Learning' and to understand how this relates to education, competence and in particular, literacy. To what extent is the 'skills revolution' improving the lives of those it is aimed at? John Payne, discussing Employee Development and Lifelong Learning, comments on the relationship to Equal Opportunities:

'If workplace learning is to make a difference it should not only contribute to the profitability of the enterprise and the revitalisation of the economy, but should provide learning opportunities for substantial sections of the workforce previously excluded from job-specific training and educational initiatives.' (Payne, 1993a:13)

Promoting basic skills provision

In her paper, A Spirit of Cordiality, Jane Mace discusses how workplace basic skills training in the UK uses the deficiency and costs to business argument. She sees this as 'a necessary tactic for funds to be released at a time when policy is market-led.' But she advises that it is important for providers to increase awareness of the impact of changing literacy demands in the workplace:

' . . .for basic skills strategies to be effective, the employees – the market for actual training, once purchased by the employer – need to be persuaded by other models than that of their own deficiencies. Learning at work, when it concerns literacy, basic education, and manual staff, means that trainers and employers have to learn, too.' (Mace, 1993:19)

As Aronowitz and Giroux explain, currently business dictates the terms of the educational debate and government supports this through policy on training. They sum up:

'Pressured by the long term decline of public revenues, uncritically influenced by the ideology of individualism, [educational institutions] have turned to increasing their ties with private resources, particularly business . . . . embracing business interests that collapse the critical into the instrumental and profitable.' (Aronowitz and Giroux, 1985:196)

Theorists point out that providers need to understand and speak the language of the New Work Order, and yet, as educators, negotiate to expand the focus of workplace education from narrow, performance oriented training for economic reasons to a broad, democratising, critical education;

'in the service of creating a public sphere of citizens who are able to exercise power over their own lives and especially over the conditions for knowledge acquisition.' (ibid)

Different skill requirements

The shift from manufacturing to service industries is said to mean an increased requirement for communications and cerebral skills. Workers with knowledge and social skills are most valued, according to management advisors. If, as Drucker suggests, 'knowledge workers' do in fact account for almost a third of the total workforce of a developed country, those whose knowledge has no currency may be particularly vulnerable.

Richard Darville echoes Zuboff's (1988) observation that workers may suffer from 'epistemological distress', a feeling that they no longer have any useful skills or knowledge, as a result of the loss of knowledge and use of manual labour, and the increased attention to symbolic controls (eg. computer monitoring of automated work processes). This effect is intensified to the extent that workplaces are 'informated' rather than 'automated' with workers 'tending data' rather than directly tending machines. (Darville, 1992: 422)

Examples of cerebral skills which have greater currency are: the ability to know equipment, troubleshoot, describe malfunction, analyse and communicate problems. There is an increased requirement to interact with print and deliver oral and written presentations (*ibid*). Workers are already expected, in order for the organisation to meet the specific requirements of quality awards, to document their responsibilities, procedures and processes, and to become familiar with new recording and auditing systems. (see Collard, 1993)

Since many of the changes that have been written about are not yet in effect, critics suggest it is important to know how far prospective client companies have progressed towards the New Work Order, and how far they intend to go. This will clarify, for the provider, the agenda of the company in terms of education and training. Does the company culture match up to the mission statement, values, statements of commitment, goals, and strategic planning? If not, this may be an opportunity for provider and management to work together to expand the education and training policy.

At any rate, it is important to become familiar with the organisation's perspective. Peter O'Connor suggests that the first step for providers is 'an exploration of the background, operations, product and industrial relations record of the company . . .' (O'Connor, 1992b:5) Laurie Field and Denis Drysdale, in their handbook for trainers and further education teachers, recommend that,

> 'to be successful, approaches to skills training within an organisation need to be grounded in . . . technocultural dimensions . . . It requires thinking about questions such as: . . . What aspects of industrial relations are related to training or the lack of it? . . . What are the implications of the structure of work groups for training and content delivery? . . . How does the organisation's technology support learning and job performance? . . . What assumptions and values are inherent in an organisation's technology and what effect do these have on training? . . . How adequate are present training approaches for developing different types of skills?' (Field and Drysdale, 1991:56)

Tony Sarmiento and Susan Schurman, speaking from a union perspective, suggest we ask if competitiveness is the compelling reason for worker education and training, if labour relations reform is necessary to workforce development, and if a job-linked literacy program is indeed the key to implementing changes. (Sarmiento and Schurman, 1992)

It is necessary to learn what the company wants from its workers. Limited problem solving or problem posing, innovative solutions and decision making? Team playing which reflects commitment and loyalty or a genuine contribution to critique and improvement? What might a contract with a particular company require providers to do on its behalf?

The effects of provision

The literature indicates that providers need to be clear about the extent to which literacy can actually change job performance, improve communications, increase company profits, improve people's lives. They need to be realistic in projecting outcomes of programmes. Strategies offered to a company need to take into account the whole organisation, Is there a positive attitude to employee development and internal promotion? Is there a communicative and democratic management style? Is literacy seen as a skill, separate from other workplace processes or as integral to all activities? Katherine Hughes takes the view that:

> '..simply improving literacy levels does little to improve the position of low paid workers.' (Hughes, 1995:108)

In negotiating with management, a cautious approach to promoting the benefits of basic skills education is advised by Mikulecky and Drew, reporting their findings in *Basic skills in the workplace*. A correlation, they say, does exist between low basic skills levels and overall job performance, but the extent of the relationship is not known:

> 'Literacy and cognitive performance do not totally explain job performance. Even the highest correlations only explain about 50% of the variance for job performance.' (Mikulecky and Drew, 1990:36,37)

The provider has a supportive and educative role to play with management in discussing the limitations isolated literacy instruction can have in improving company profits. The literature demonstrates that the links between literacy and increased competitiveness are tenuous.

Looking back at change within the organisation over a long period of time and at how people have responded to this change, eg. through peer learning and pooling of knowledge, could be useful in countering employer beliefs about individual deficits. One way of opening up the debate about what counts as appropriate literacies is to bring together workers across different sectors of an organisation, so revealing contradictions in the definitions. (Thanks to Catherine Macrae, team leader of the City of Edinburgh Adult Basic Education Community Education Programme, for her comments.)

Management can be made aware of other strategies to improve profitability. For example: clearer communications, increased cultural sensitivity, greater attention to workers' health and safety, greater worker participation in the choice and design of education programmes and company changes. A more participatory model of workplace education is called for, with all stakeholders, including the workers posing problems and finding solutions. (Compare Jurmo and Fingeret, 1989; Gowen, 1990; Darville, 1992.)

Worker resistance

Theorists warn literacy education providers in the workplace of the need to be aware that workers may well already possess many of the new communication skills demanded by the New Work Order, and be using them effectively in contexts outside the workplace. Examples are explored in Gowen (1990) and Barton and Hamilton (1998) and unvalued and undervalued skills need to be acknowledged in the negotiation and implementation of programmes.

Gowen's research illustrates the danger of worker resistance to training programmes where they have not been consulted, where their existing skills have not been taken into account, where learning seems meaningless and irrelevant to actual workplace and social practices, and where 'learning' is not learning, but a process of gaining recognition for prior knowledge.

In her work with Emerald Manufacturing, literacy assessments of front line workers showed low literacy skills, which management perceived as a crisis. Management were persuaded to recognise the high level of oral and problem solving skills the workers did possess, and that productivity improvements would need more than literacy skills development. (Gowen, 1996)

Critical literacy in the workplace

Providers can be confident in promoting an expanded concept of literacy: the ability to think critically can be evidenced as a valued attribute. The writings of management consultants such as Tom Peters, Peter Senge and Peter Drucker, predict skills and knowledge that will be required of all workers. These can be linked to a Freirean concept of critical literacy.

Stephen Brookfield, in his book *Developing Critical Thinkers*, comments:

> *'In workplace settings where democratic participation and worker control are the norm, the conditions for critical thinking are favourable.' (Brookfield, 1987:139)*

As Keith Forrester, John Payne and Kevin Ward have shown in their study of workplace learning, an open and democratic attitude towards employee development will have flow-on benefits from worker appreciation resulting in a greater willingness to participate. (Forrester *et al*, 1995)

References

Social science theory

Aronowitz, S. and Giroux, H. (1985). *Education Under Siege: The Conservative, Liberal and Radical Debate over Schooling*. South Hadley, Massachusetts: Bergin and Garvey.

Aronowitz, S. and DiFazio, W. (1994). *The Jobless Future*. Minneapolis: University of Minnesota Press.

Barton, D. and Hamilton, M. (1998) *Local Literacies: Reading and Writing in One Community*. London: Routledge.

Brookfield, S. (1987). *Developing Critical Thinkers: Challenging adults to explore alternative ways of thinking and acting*. San Francisco: Jossey-Bass.

Cornfield, D. (1987). *Workers, Managers, and Technological Change*. New York: Plenum Press

Darville, R. (1992). The Economic Push for Literacy: Expansive or Restrictive? In *Proceedings of Adult Literacy: An International Urban Perspective*. New York: UNESCO

Fingeret, H. (1988). *The Politics of Literacy: Choices for the Coming Decade*. Keynote address, Literacy Volunteers of America Conference. Albuquerque: New Mexico:

Forrester, K., Payne, J. and Ward, K. (1995). *Workplace Learning*. Aldershot: Avebury, Ashgate Publishing Ltd.

Freebody, P. and Welch, A. (1993). Individualisation and Domestication in Current Literacy Debates in Australia. In Freebody, P. and Welch, A. Eds. *Knowledge, Culture and Power: International Perspectives on Literacy as Policy and Practice*. Bristol: Falmer Press.

Gee, J. P. (1994a). *New Alignments and Old Literacies: From Fast Capitalism to the Canon*. Carlton: Australian Reading Association.

Gee, J.P. (1994b). Quality, Science and the Lifeworld *Critical Forum*. 3, 1. Leichhardt: ALBSAC.

Gee, J., Hull, G. and Lankshear, C. (1996). *The New Work Order* . St. Leonards NSW: Allen and Unwin.

Gowen, S.G.(1990). *Eyes on a Different Prize: A Critical Ethnography of a Workplace Literacy Program*. Atlanta: unpublished manuscript, Georgia State University.

Gowen, S.G. (1992). *The Politics of Workplace Literacy*. New York: Teachers College Press.

Gowen, S.G. (1996). How the Reorganisation of Work Destroys Everyday Knowledge, in Hautecoeur, J. P. (Ed.) *Basic Education and Work: Alpha 96*. Toronto: UNESCO and Culture Concepts.

Graff, H. (1986). *The Legacies of Literacy: Continuities and Contradictions in Western Culture and Society*. Bloomington Indiana: Indiana University Press.

Hughes, K. (1995). Really Useful Knowledge. In Mayo, M. and Thompson, J, Eds. *Adult Learning, Critical Intelligence and Social Change*. Leicester: NIACE.

Hull, G. (1991a). *Examining the Relations of Literacy to Vocational Education and Work: An Ethnography of a Vocational Program in Banking and Finance*. Berkeley: University of California.

Hull, G. (1994). Hearing Other Voices: A Critical Assessment of Popular Views of Literacy and Work, In O'Connor, P. Ed. *Thinking Work*. Sydney: ALBSAC

Luke, A. (1992). Literacy and Work in 'New Times.'. *Open Letter, 3* (1).

Mace, J. (1992a). Love, Literacy and Labour. *Research and Practice in Adult Literacy*, Vol. 17 (Spring).

Mace, J (1993) 'A Spirit of Cordiality' Learning at Work: Perspectives and Participants. In Machell, J. and Frank, F. Eds. *Learning at Work: Collected Papers* Lancaster: Centre for the Study of Education and Training, Lancaster University.

Marsick, V.J. Ed. *Learning in the Workplace*. Beckenham, Kent: Croom Helm.

O'Connor, P. (1992b). *Making it Happen: Developing Effective Workplace Basic Skills Training Programs*. Leichhardt: ALBSAC.

O'Connor, P. (1994). *Thinking Work*. Leichhardt: ALBSAC.

Saunders, M. (1995a). The Integrative Principle: Higher Education and Work–based Learning in the UK. *European Journal of Education*. 30 (2). Paris: European Institute of Education and Social Policy.

Turk, J. (1990). *Literacy: Defining the Problem, Posing the Solution*. Halifax: Canadian Vocational Association Conference.

Turk, J. and Unda, J. (1991). So We Can Make our Voices Heard: The Ontario Federation of Labour's BEST project on Worker Literacy. in Taylor, M. Lewe, G. and Draper, J., Eds. *Basic Skills for the Workplace* Toronto: Culture Concepts.

Zuboff, S. (1988) *In the Age of the Smart Machine*. New York: Basic Books.

Management texts

Australian Chamber of Manufacturers. (1991) *Australian Chamber of Manufacturers: Education and Training Policy*.

Boyett, J. H. and Conn, H. P. (1992). *Workplace 2000: The Revolution Reshaping American Business*. New York: Plume Penguin.

Business Council for Effective Literacy. (1988). *Functional Illiteracy Hurts Business*. New York: BCEL

Business Council for Effective Literacy. (1993). The Connection Between Employee Basic Skills and Productivity. *Workforce and Workplace Literacy Series*, 8 (March). New York: BCEL

Collard, R. (1993). *Total Quality Success through People*. London: Institute of Personnel Management.

Confederation of British Industry. (1989). *Towards a Skills Revolution*. London: CBI.

Drucker, P. F. (1993). *Post-Capitalist Society*. New York: Harper.

Johnson, W.B. and Packer, A.E. (1987). *Workforce 2000: Work and Workers in the 21st Century* New York: Hudson Institute.

Omega. (1989). *Literacy in the Workplace: The Executive Perspective*. Bryn Mawr: Omega Group.

Reich, R. (1992). *The Work of Nations*. New York: New York Vintage Books.

Sticht, T., McDonald, B. and Hule, C. (1992). *Getting WELL: Workforce Education and Lifelong Learning*. San Diego: Applied Behavioural and Cognitive Sciences Inc.

Wiggenhorn, W. (1990). Motorola U: When Training Becomes Education. *Harvard Business Review*, (July-August).

Policy documents

Department of Education, Employment and Training [DEET]. (1991). *Australia's Language: The Australian Language and Literacy Policy. Companion Volume to the Policy Paper*. Canberra: Australian Government Publishing Service Australia

Department of Trade and Industry (1994). *Competitiveness: Helping Businesses to Win*. London: HMSO CM2563

Drouin, M. J. (1990). *Workforce Literacy: An Economic Challenge for Canada.*. Montreal: Hudson Institute.

Education and Training Support Agency. (1993). *Taking the Step to Skill New Zealand*. Wellington: ETSA and New Zealand Qualifications Authority.

Harman, D. and Lerche, R. (1988). *The Bottom Line: Basic Skills in the Workplace*. New York: US Department of Education, US Department of Labor.

Keating, P. (1994). *Working Nation: The White Paper on Employment and Growth*. Canberra: Australian Government Publishing Service.

Reports

Adult Literacy and Basic Skills Unit. (1995a). *The Cost to Industry: Basic Skills and the UK Workforce*. London: ALBSU

Adult Literacy and Basic Skills Unit. (1995b). *Basic Skills Training at Work: A Study of Effectiveness* London: ALBSU.

Atkinson, J and Spilsbury, M. (1993) *Basic Skills and Jobs*. London: ALBSU/ BSA.

Carnevale, A.P. Gainer, L.J. and Meltzer, A.S. (1990). *Workplace Basics: the Skills Employers Want*. Washington DC: US Department of Labor, American Society for Training and Development.

Confederation of British Industry (1989). *Towards a Skills Revolution*. London: CBI.

Mikulecky, L. and Drew, R. (1990). Basic Skills in the Workplace. *Constructs of Reader Process*. Unpublished manuscript. USA.

Moore, L. and Benseman, J. (1993). *Literacy at Work: An exploratory Survey of Literacy and Basic Education Needs in the Workplace*. Auckland: ARLA Workbase.

Payne, J. (1993a) Employee Development and Lifelong Learning. In Machell, J and Frank, F. Eds. *Learning at Work: Collected Papers*. Lancaster: Lancaster University.

Wickert, R. (1989). *No Single Measure: A Survey of Australian Adult Literacy*. Sydney: Institute of Technical and Adult Teacher Education, Sydney College of Advanced Education.

World Economic Forum. (1989). *World Competitiveness Report*. World Economic Forum and the IMEDE.

Unions

Cornfield, D. (1987). *Workers, Managers, and Technological Change*. New York: Plenum Press.

Sarmiento, T. and Schurman, S. (1992). *A Job Linked Literacy Program for SPC: Are We Talking About Worker Training, Work Reorganisation, or More Equitable Workplaces?* Michigan: Work in America Institute.

Current practice/Guidelines

Collins, S. (1989). Workplace Literacy: Corporate Tool or Worker Empowerment? *Social Policy* Vol. 20, 1,Summer 1989. New York: City University.

Field, L. and Drysdale, D. (1991). *Training for Competence* . London: Kogan Page.

Jurmo, P. and Fingeret, H., Eds. (1989). *Participatory Literacy Education* San Francisco: Jossey-Bass.

Stein, S. G. (1991) *Workplace Literacy and the Transformation of the American Workplace: A Model for Effective Practice*. Montreal: Paper presented at the Annual Meeting of the American Association for Adult and Continuing Education.

High performance workplaces

TQM and change

Total quality management is seen by some education theorists and practitioners as being a potential ally in advocating the benefits of workplace education, and this is largely because of the way it links itself to democratic practices. Management texts presented here will outline their view of the world and the ideal worker/workplace. The comments of critics will be included.

Democratic workplaces

Total Quality Management [TQM] is the management style which introduced and supports this new 'fast capitalist' work order. It claims to serve the interests of workers as well as management by dismantling rigid hierarchies, introducing egalitarian participative management and problem solving. Peter Drucker writes in *Post-Capitalist Society*:

> *'The task of the knowledge-based organisation is not to make everybody a boss. It is to make everybody a contributor.' (Drucker, 1993:109)*

The contribution that all employees are able to make, he claims, allows post-capitalist organisations to be more socially responsible than those driven only by economic performance (*ibid*:101–108)

Change and turmoil

TQM and high performance organisations require that workers within them accept rapid change as inevitable and necessary. Drucker prescribes:

> *'Every organisation of today has to build into its very structure the management of change.' (ibid:59)*

This, he says, requires continuous improvement, exploitation of past successes and innovation, and the necessary destabilisation and transcendence of communities. Tom Peters, management consultant, goes further:

> *'Forget change! The word is feeble. Keep saying "revolution." '*
>
> *(Peters, 1994:8)*

Workers are encouraged to accept that their time in any organisation is likely to be short-lived. Helen Rainbird comments:

> *' . . . now and in the future workers will be expected to adapt and/ or change their jobs continuously in their lives. Training is expected to be pivotal in this process.' (Rainbird, 1990:65)*

Gee *et al* add:

> '*workers must be 'eager to stay' but also 'ready to leave' if the business is failing . . .*' (Gee et al, 1996:19)

Zero defects

TQM, according to the Institute of Personnel Management in the UK,

> ' *. . . can be defined as zero defects in the products and services provided by an organisation in order to satisfy customer needs.*' (Collard, 1993)

The American company Motorola U aims at 99.99966% defect-free production, referred to by statisticians as 'six sigma', an ideal which they have not yet reached. (Wiggenhorn, 1990:74) Every function in the organisation is seen to have a series of suppliers and customers, internal and external, which must be satisfied. International standards (BS5750, ISO9000 series) set out how organisations can establish, maintain and document an effective quality system. (Collard, 1993)

All work operations are standardised to reduce variation in process and quality, production is continuously improved, and non-value added labour is eliminated.

Training is introduced:

> '*Investment in training is a critical factor in the success of a total quality programme; it requires all levels to be involved and to attend, compulsorily, without excuse.*' (ibid, 1993).

Taking the people with you

Each person in the workplace is a part of the 'quality chain', which comprises quality circles, a team of four to twelve people usually from the same work area, who meet on a regular basis to identify, investigate, analyse and solve their work related problems. Such meetings of 'quality circles' or 'teams', have also been referred to in the trade union literature as 'co-operation apparatus.' (Parker and Slaughter, 1994) Steve Wilkinson, in his guide for practitioners, expands:

> '*The idea is that all staff get involved in looking at their work and in thinking of better ways of doing things. In Japan, this is often cross departmental but is less so in the UK. These circles can only work if management can motivate the workforce to feel ownership of the product and pride in their role . . . The earliest Quality Circles included a literacy and general education element . . . easy to read pamphlets were developed which contained Quality principles . . . the workers read and discussed these simple texts, which developed literacy and quality skills simultaneously.*' (Wilkinson, 1994:7)

Businesses see the need to institute reform which engages 'the skills, education and energy of your workforce.' Chris Leavy, of Toyota [Thames, NZ] explains:

> 'You have to take the people with you, because only the guy who does the job can load the quality in.' (quoted in Young, 1992)

Training encourages workers to take on the goals and vision of the organisation as her or his own:

> 'To be effective in an organisation, employees need to have a sense of how organisation works and how the activities of each individual affect organisational and strategic objectives.' (Carnevale et al, 1990:34)

Shared vision

Peter Senge describes the concept of a 'shared vision.':

> 'In a corporation, a shared vision changes people's relationship with the company. It is no longer 'their company', it becomes 'our company.' . . . It creates a common identity.' (Senge, 1990:208)

He adds:

> 'Shared visions compel courage so naturally that people don't even recognise the extent of their courage. Courage is simply doing whatever is needed in pursuit of the vision.' (ibid:208)

Shared vision is essential for gaining the commitment of individuals to the long term view. (ibid:210) With a combination of 'shared vision' and 'knowledge', the worker, at any level of the workforce, would then have the 'courage' to do the work that was once the responsibility of management: to try new ways of thinking and acting, to take risks and experiment. He or she would have the courage to utilise high level problem solving and communication skills with individuals and in teams in order to increase profits for the organisation.

James Paul Gee sees the shared vision of the Quality Discourse as:

> ' . . . a yet more 'advanced' sort of hegemony in which 'workers' [now 'partners'] actively choose under coercion . . . The consequences of not making this choice – and this [TQ] literature is overt about this, too – is to exit the post capitalist world and end up in a dead end and low paid 'service' job.' (Gee, 1994b:14)

The critics

Gee, in *Quality, Science, and the Lifeworld*, calls the articulation of this new capitalism by business and academics, 'the Quality Discourse.' (Gee, 1994b:6) The goals of this Discourse emphasise quality rather than profit. Indeed:

> 'The ideology of the new capitalism claims that the goal, vision, or purpose of a successful business cannot merely be profit. This simply won't motivate all workers/partners to commit themselves fully . . .' (Gee et al, 1996:20)

Gee shows how language is used to hegemonise, and uses the term 'Enchanted Workers of the Quality Discourse' (Gee et al, 1996:25). Such use of language, he says, can alter the way workers perceive their place at work, and becomes a management tool for motivating workers to assume responsibilities for production and service that used to belong to middle management (Gee, 1994). Examples include 'self direction' and 'empowerment' (Lankshear, 1994), managers who are 'project directors', 'team leaders.' and 'facilitators.' (Gee 1994b) or even 'designers' (Senge, 1990:341). Workers may be referred to as 'partners' (Gee, 1994, Frank and Hamilton, 1993).

These and other similar terms are deployed by management to create a sense of democracy and individual power, where it may not in fact exist (Boyett and Conn, 1992, Senge, 1990, Peters 1992). The terms are also reflected in policy papers (New Zealand Qualifications Authority 'Quality' conference papers 1993).

Gowen explains:

> 'While management wants workers to become more 'empowered' to make decisions and solve problems, they generally still want ultimate control over the content of those decisions and solutions. So, the question they are really asking is: 'How do you 'empower' workers to increase their skills in order to increase corporate profits?' Rather than say, how do you 'empower' workers to increase their skills to reshape the distributions of power for a more democratic workplace?' (Gowen, 1996:15)

Gowen accepts the theoretical possibility that TQ

> 'could mean changes to more democratic workplaces with shared governance . . .' (Gowen, 1996:13)

However, she disagrees that there is generally any attempt at greater democracy. She quotes Huey, 1994:

> 'While the discourse of Total Quality includes a strong emphasis on worker empowerment and flattened hierarchies, some experts predict that only about five percent of all workplaces actually accomplish those ends.' (Huey, quoted in Gowen, 1996:14)

Flexibility

Flexibility has been presented in much of the management literature as either the ability of workers to exercise more autonomy over the labour process, or as a way of describing or masking practices which enable firms to exercise control over labour. Flexible work practices such as multiskilling, upskilling, staggered and reduced work hours are marketed as beneficial both to workers and management, yet critics question the real fate of skills in this regime. The paradox of rigid competencies is evidenced, as is the effect of 'flexibility' on labour strength.

Veronica McGivney, in her report on the *Wasted Potential* of 'atypical' workers [those not in full time employment], reports this comment:

> '*According to one employer: 'flexible working practices are business-driven, not welfare-driven' (Dow Stoker, quoted in McGivney 1994:5)*

She adds:

> '*Several analysts have pointed out that flexible working is a one way concept that furthers the employers' interests to a greater extent than the employee' (ibid:5)*

She records another opinion:

> '*The motive force encouraging greater flexibility has been the desire for productivity gains, not gains in work-family harmonisation nor gender equality.' (quoting McRae, ibid:5)*

Others who see flexibility as a strategy for extending managerial control, include Pollert (1987) and O'Connor (1994).

Benefits or restrictions?

Although the management literature promotes the benefits of part time work and flexible working hours to workers, others are concerned about restricted opportunities (see, for instance, Forrester *et al*, 1995). The *New York Times* (Dec 1992) comments:

> '*Employment agencies call them contingent workers. Some labor economists, by contrast, call them disposable and throwaway workers.' (quoted in Aronowitz and DiFazio 1994:1).*

Brooks maintains that while there can be a downside, the benefits of flexibility for some workers may be increased through technological decentralisation. That is, some may be able to work from home, with the concomitant loss of control by the employer (Brooks, 1990:37–46).

Multiskilling and upskilling

'Flexibility' is also promoted to support arguments for multiskilling. However, where workers are trained across a range of tasks within a particular company there is little evidence as yet that these skills can be transferred to other companies in the same industrial sector (Rainbird, 1990:90–118) and therefore little evidence of specific benefits to workers. In fact the range of tasks often involves lower skill levels, due to technological advances, and correspondingly lower wages. In the new management literature, flexibility is also couched as a desirable *attitude* for workers to possess. It can even be seen as a basic skill to be developed:

> '*Workers need to be more flexible . . . workers with poor basic skills will be ill-equipped for any change.' (Harman and Lerche, 1988)*

The acquisition of these attitudes is said to enhance worker co-operation.

Skill degradation?

Skill degradation can occur when workplaces put organisational flexibility before skill. Either less skilled workers may be hired who possess the right attitudes [adaptability to an increased workload and lower wages], and/or technology which makes skill redundant will be introduced. Braverman records this phenomenon in the printing industry (1974) and Aronowitz and DiFazio (1994) observe the current lower skill levels of a checkout operator, where electronic checking devices are used to scan and price products. Such examples challenge the received view, such as in a 1986 OECD report, quoted By Drouin:

> 'Managers repeatedly underlined that the development of teamwork and the emergence of new jobs at the interface of traditionally distinct functions has created new needs for workers with broad competence profiles and multiple skills, reaching from polyvalent team workers to "flexible specialists".' (Drouin, 1990:18)

In *Training Matters*, Rainbird surveys trade union experiences and reports:

> 'Many trade union officials reported casualisation, job losses and deskilling rather than the existence of training programmes enhancing skills.' (Rainbird 1990:118)

Flexible work hours

The disadvantages for workers, particularly those who are not part of the (diminishing) core workforce, are numerous:

> 'the growing peripheral workforce experience 'the 'flexibility' of weakened bargaining positions, lower wages, less but staggered hours of work, less work-related benefits, less job security, fewer career options, and fewer opportunities to access education and training.' (O'Connor, 1994:17)

Brooks notes the growing demand for flexibility amongst Australian employers and comments:

> 'This was highlighted by the disputes in the 1980s over the introduction of night work and weekend work (including Sunday) in the retail trading industry; and the introduction of continuous shift work in the mining industry.' (Brooks, 1990:4)

Flexible attitudes and working in teams

Teams, or quality circles, widely accepted and utilised by organisations employing total quality procedures, expose some of the inconsistencies of management policy. In what Gee, Hull and Lankshear (1996) call the 'paradox of flexibility', TQM claims to want to encourage team decision making, problem solving, increased responsibility and continuous improvement.

And yet motivation becomes a problem in the face of other less worker friendly 'flexible' policies such as 'downsizing' and decreased job security. Gee explains:

> 'Business cannot succeed today without all workers fully buying into the ends/ goals/vision of the organisation. They must pro-actively take responsibility . . . This will only happen if workers choose to believe in the ends . . . but at the same time these ends . . . are set by visionary leaders . . . not by the workers . . . If the workers don't 'buy into them', they are 'out'. This is, then, an odd form of choice, and, indeed, an odd form of 'empowerment' . . .' (Gee, 1994b:13)

The requirement to be a good 'team player' can also interfere with the critical thinking and action necessary for problem solving. Brookfield quotes Victoria Marsick (1987) who reports on the testimony of the presidential commission after the explosion shortly after launch of the American space shuttle *Challenger*:

> 'No one wished to voice his or her concerns about safety, for fear of appearing troublesome or not being a 'team player.' Marsick argues that workers have been so conditioned not to raise questions that they may not know how to begin to think critically.' (Brookfield, 1987:137)

Inflexible competencies

A further paradox is contained in the drive for competency based training, which is inflexible and individualistic, within organisations encouraging cooperative working practices such as teams. (compare Toms, 1995, Forrester et al, 1995) Schultz points out:

> ' . . . while U.S. companies are introducing new forms of work organisation, with new participation structures and patterns of interaction, many are choosing to teach and evaluate their employees with traditional (Taylorist) methods. Reorganised companies are asking workers to become active learners in the workplace and passive students in the classroom.' (Schultz, 1992:iv)

Referring to Mintzberg, Burgoyne comments on the controlling function of 'flexibility.':

> ' . . . standardisation of skill is one of the main ways of achieving control in a human setting – people can only be what they do.' (Burgoyne, 1993:3)

Legislation

Helen Rainbird points out that the state has had a significant part to play in the achievement of labour flexibility where deregulation has occurred. Discussing the UK, she notes:

> 'It has done this through changes in employment rights and social security legislation as well as through a determined attack on trade union organisation.' (Rainbird, 1990:92)

She quotes the European Trade Union Institute, who argue:

> *'The goal of some advocates of 'flexibility' has become not just the removal of legislation regulating the use of labour at company level, but the fundamental weakening of trade unions' ability to represent their members' interests and take action to advance them.' (ibid:93)*

The impact of technology

Technology has a powerful effect on work organisation and culture, and therefore on our understanding of workplace literacy. Texts selected here discuss the positive and negative effects of technology on work and workers. Skill enhancement, as well as disempowerment, deskilling and displacement arguments are outlined.

Transformative technology

Information Technology is a term that encompasses a variety of hardware and software configurations. It is hitting the industrialised world with speed. A 1984 Swedish study revealed that one out of four workers were using computers in their work (quoted in Burton, 1992:14). Kristen Nygaard, writing in 1980 to inform New Zealand unions about the lessons learned from the Norwegian experience, points out:

> *'The advantages to management of the recent development in information technology are obvious in terms of opportunities for increased productivity, new products, an improved information base for decision making and tighter control of the use of labour, capital, and raw materials.' (Nygaard, 1980:9)*

Nell Eurich, author of a Carnegie Foundation Special Report on Corporate Classrooms, is optimistic about the effect of technology:

> *'Literally millions of new jobs have been created in America because of high technology and its applications. People are either working at new jobs or they are working in entirely new industries . . . And every industry from banking to utilities to sales will require men and women who are technologically up-to-date.' (Eurich, 1985:11)*

The rapid evolution of new technologies, optimists believe, has a positive transformative effect on the organisation of the workplace and on industrial democracy. Brooks expands:

> *'The optimists see questions of industrial democracy (that is, workers having a greater say in the organisation of their jobs) as an automatic consequence of introducing new technologies.' (Brooks, 1990:17)*

Computerisation at all levels

New technology pervades workplaces such as those involved with production, service and retail. It has been said to have a certain levelling effect in that workers and management alike are having to retrain in this area. David Hood, former Chief Executive of the New Zealand Qualifications Authority, comments in an interview:

> 'Around the world new technology is blurring the boundaries . . . Once manual labourers (in a steel mill) would have handled the molten metal. Now there's an operator working on a computer directing the whole operation.' (cited in Brown and Hubrich, 1995)

Tasks once performed by typists and secretaries are now performed by executives either on home computers or at the workplace. According to Cornfield, technology has transfromed occupations, creating new skills and destroying others, altered the power relationships between workers and managers and changed the way workers learn and work. (Cornfield, 1987)

Outwork

Computer technology has had an impact on the number of people working from home. In fact, profitable enterprises show companies how to 'outwork' their employees to save time, space and money. Benefits to workers are cited: the freedom to work from home, avoid traffic congestion, and be based in one's local community. Brooks sees this as positive in that this gives the worker a measure of independence, and allows her/him more control over work processes. (Brooks, 1990:17) Aronowitz and DiFazio (somewhat reservedly) report Piore and Sabel's argument against the view that technology deskills:

> 'the new computer technologies create the possibility for the reemergence of a new regime of craft production. For them this is a result of a flexible specialisation, decentralised, community-based, small-batch, skilled worker production process' (Aronowitz and DiFazio, 1994: 90)

Disempowerment

Aronowitz and DiFazio present a strongly contrasting viewpoint. The utilisation of technology for profit and accompanying disempowerment of workers at all levels is discussed in *The Jobless Future*:

> 'The new technoculture in the workplace emerges on the ruins of the old, mechanical, industrial culture. From the perspective of the worker, whether in the factory or the office, the second phase of automatic production – computerization – is merely a wrinkle in the long process of disempowerment.' (ibid:85)

Probert and Wajcman support this general view:

' . . . *whereas post-industrial theorists see such work as 'part of a positive future',*
for others it evokes the ugly spectre of 'sweated' self-exploitative piecework' with
virtually no autonomy and strictly minimal prospects for innovation, creativity,
personal development and challenge.' (Probert and Wajcman 1988:436)

Nygaard cites social isolation of workers and the resulting effect of lack of community on union strength as a further example of disempowerment. (Nygaard,
1980:4) This point is underlined by Robert Burns, author of *The Adult Learner at*
Work:

' . . . *while some tiring, repetitive jobs have been eliminated, new technology has*
contributed to the loss of old skills and decreased job satisfaction through social
isolation.' (Burns, 1995:9)

Displacement

Cornfield claims the introduction of technology has created large scale
'technological unemployment', resulting in a shift from union collective
bargaining for shorter working hours to a call for training and retraining for
displaced employees. (Cornfield, 1987) Aronowitz and DiFazio argue that the
qualifications required by computers have created new opportunities for
satisfying well paid jobs for a few. But most experience further subordination,
displacement, irrelevance.

'*Displacement is a continuous process, and all levels of workers, from unskilled to*
engineers and managers, will be deskilled. Machinery and new forms of organisa-
tion will replace skilled work, creating permanent tendencies of structural
unemployment.' (Aronowitz and Di Fazio, 1994:91)

Brooks backs this up:

'*The committee of Inquiry into Technological Change in Australia found that*
jobless growth would occur in many areas of work and that new technology would
increase the absolute number of skilled tasks and decrease the number of unskilled
tasks. In other words, unskilled workers would be most affected by technological
change. This trend explains why trade unions have pressed for shorter working
hours and a sharing of the volume of available work.' (Brooks, 1990:18)

Contracting technological services off-site and even off-shore is cheaper than
developing technology at the workplace, and thus workers are further displaced.
(compare Rainbird, 1990; Cornfield, 1987; Aronowitz and DiFazio, 1994)

Examples of job displacement can be found in the public service sector
as well as in private sector organisations. Reports such as this, in the *NZ*
Herald (2/4/97) no longer surprise:

'*The Minister of Police said that . . . 540 jobs had to be axed to fund the*
multimillion dollar crime fighting computer system, Incis.'

Reducing skill requirements.

It is maintained that technology demands higher level skills: executives complain that they are held back not by inadequate technology,

> '. . but by the ability of the organisation to provide competent service personnel to work with that technology.' (Omega 1989:8)

The effect that technology has had in increasing literacy requirements in the workplace is underlined by educators:

> 'The central thrust of the post-industrial economy with its dramatic technological advances calls for higher order literacies to be much more widespread in the population than ever before.' (Levett and Lankshear, 1994:2)

The case against technology as an agent in increasing and expanding craft skills is strong, however. Bailey (1990) explains the life cycle theory of technological change, first advanced by James Bright:

> ' . . . that advanced skills were required by new technologies, but once a technology matured, the skills needed to work, operate and maintain it fell.' (Bailey, 1990:7)

However, it is not simply technology that is responsible for loss of jobs, or even for deskilling. Braverman claims it is used simply for profit:

> 'Science is the last – and after labor the most important – social property to be turned into an adjunct of capital.' (Braverman, 1974: 156)

Braverman's work attacks post-modernist workplaces for the way technology is used to reduce skills needed by production workers, while increasing skills for managers and planners (ibid:236–247). Helen Rainbird, writing from a union perspective, advises:

> 'It is extremely difficult to assess the 'effect' of new technology in isolation, without reference to the complex social systems into which it is being introduced.' (Rainbird, 1990:68)

A great number of literacy programmes in the workplace aim to develop computer literacy for workers, yet some findings reveal that:

> ' . . . in many instances, new technology is introduced in such as way as to reduce skill requirements . . . a large number of jobs are disappearing or being radically modified by it . . .' (ibid:88)

Darville notes that workers have experienced a loss of knowledge, having now to use the computer's information about a product, rather than the knowledge gained from years of contact with it. (Darville, 1992:417–419) In answer to suggestions that a job may be 'upskilled' in terms of literacy while being 'deskilled' in terms of craft, a striking example is provided by Thomas Bailey in his discussion of technology, work organisations, jobs and tasks:

'*In many outlets, standard cash registers with numbered buttons have been replaced by machines that have little pictures of hamburgers and french fries printed on the keys. This could be the ultimate example of deskilling.*' (Bailey, 1990:9)

Finally, Burns advises:

'*We can and must use new technology to develop flexible, multiskilled teams where jobs are varied and employees have discretion, so that we expand the technical skills of employees. The effective use of new technology requires a workforce that uses a high level of initiative and involves itself in proactive, problem-solving behaviour.*' (Burns, 1995: 10)

Core and periphery workers

This chapter lays out the arguments posed mostly by critical theorists, concerned with the erosion of rights, including access to training, when workers who have been made peripheral to their employers' needs and the workforce is trimmed to its core.

Loss of full-time, permanent work

Structural changes in employment patterns (part-time, casual, temporary, intermittent) are illustrated in the 'Shamrock' pattern of employment, showing the segmented hierarchy of the workforce directly or indirectly employed by a big company (Kumazawa and Yamada, 1989, quoted in O'Connor, 1993:13). It emphasises the distinction between core and periphery workers, and between employment contracts and sub-contractors and other self employed persons. Canadians Jean-Marc Fontan and Eric Shragge comment:

'*Around a core of well-paid regular employees receiving significant social benefits, a growing number of people who are less well paid hover on the fringes, with no social security benefits and permanent job status. These occasional workers are a pool of resources available to private, public and cooperative enterprises to expand or contract their operations in response to the economic situation of the moment.*' (Fontan and Schragge, 1996:280)

Katherine Hughes points out that in Britain:

'*Between June 1978 and June 1993, 2.9 million full-time jobs disappeared with 1.4 million part-time jobs developing in the same time.*' (Hughes, 1995:100)

Erosion of rights

O'Connor states that the growing peripheral workforce is experiencing:

'*the 'flexibility' of weakened bargaining positions, lower wages, less but staggered hours of work, less work-related benefits, less job security, fewer career options, and fewer opportunities to access education and training.*' (O'Connor, 1994:17)

It is becoming more commonplace for people to be employed by an organisation on a full time basis with the expectation that they will provide their own office space and resources, i.e. work from home. The core is shrinking, the periphery expanding.

'. . . it is likely that in the near future the law, and society at large, will talk simply of contracts for the performance of work.' (Brooks, 1990:45)

The question of rights for periphery workers, including the right to training and education, has been explored by a number of authors. (Forrester, 1995; Tuckett, 1991; Atkinson, 1988; Pollert, 1987; Mace and Wolfe, 1988)

Regarding women

Pollert claims that this core-periphery dualism merely extends and intensifies labour market segregation by gender, race and age, and Jane Mace points out that most periphery workers are women and 'minorities'. She further explains that women often take jobs which do not utilise, or challenge, the abilities they have. The 'choices' of such women focus on arrangements that can be made for child care and hours of work. The jobs frequently require minimal literacy skills.

Mace and Wolfe's argument is supported by Toms who notes that 'flexibility' claims to increase opportunity for women [part-time work, flexible hours], but has the power to further entrench the inequalities (Toms, 1995: 50–54).

Some implications for provision

TQM and change

Helen Rainbird refers to the changes accompanying Total Quality Management as 'the homogenisation of working culture' (Rainbird, 1990:115). She warns of the affect of extensive training programmes which, she says, have reduced the right of individual workers to particular jobs on the basis of specialist skills. Where employees have similar skills it is easier for employers to justify redundancies.

Quality circles and being a 'Team Player' are key components of the quality movement. A report on *The Skills Employers Want* states:

'Change strategies are usually dependent on the ability of employees to pull together and refocus on the new common goal.' (Carnevale et al, 1990:32)

Where, under old-style capitalism, workers were not required to think, under the new capitalism workers are now required to think, but only in a certain way. Where 'total quality' involves the requirement that workers accept, unquestioningly, organisational changes, critical awareness is forestalled. Compliance and motivation to pursue corporate goals may be the expected outcomes of programmes.

This has important implications for literacy provision. In attempting to address the needs of the organisation, providers may collude in bringing about a 'homogenised working culture' with a common viewpoint and a common goal, in which those who want to retain a different viewpoint and a separate identity, are 'dropped off.' Where organisations genuinely aim for democracy and self management by workers, Brookfield explains that in order to succeed, critical thinking is essential:

> 'Workers need to learn how to obtain, understand, and apply information traditionally reserved only for managers. Quality circle leaders and participants need some acquaintance with a broad range of skills, including those of critical thinking, group dynamics and problem solving. Workers in plants in which new technologies are being considered need to be involved in the selection and introduction of these innovations. When workers are involved in strategic decisions at the highest policy levels, they must be able to understand and challenge corporate financial reports and management proposals.' (Brookfield, 1987:149)

The suggestion here is that providers should convince client organisations who are serious about democratic self management, of the necessity to facilitate and encourage the development of critical thinking.

The goal of flexibility

Often seen by management as part of workplace basic skills, the 'attribute' of flexibility may be simply the ability to see others' points of view and to work cooperatively with them, while still maintaining (and being able to state) one's own viewpoint. These are useful attributes for teamwork.

However, in the New Work Order, workers must be multiskilled and upskilled to perform a greater variety of tasks, or to take on responsibilities of other now redundant personnel. Helen Rainbird observes that new technology and flexible working practices are often introduced in the absence of formal training programmes, and that this decreases flexibility for workers. (Rainbird, 1990:172). She maintains further that:

> 'Training cannot be analysed in isolation from the employment relationship and must of necessity be examined in relation to industrial policy and the general political and economic environment ' (ibid:173)

Often literacy provision is requested as a tag-on to other workplace training an development initiatives. This does not allow examination of the impact of technology and flexible working practices, nor does it take account of industrial relations issues. Such provision may be self-defeating in that it is at best of no real use to the workers it targets, and at worst, is harmful to their interests.

Resistance to adjustability

Flexibility may become 'adjustability' in the context of the new workplace:

> 'Important to workers engaging willingly in workplace reform, is the creation of education and training within workplaces, to ensure that the philosophy and direction of reforms are clearly understood at all levels.' (Young, 1992)

Flexibility is promoted as empowering for workers. Gowen asks what kind of 'literacy' do organisations, claiming to 'empower' their workers, require? And answers that it is more likely to be a 'docility certificate' than 'critical literacy and civic courage'. (Gowen, 1996:15)

When 'flexibility' is seen by management as the ability of workers to adjust, the attempt to develop such 'skills' in workers often fails. Sheryl Gowen and others researching in the workplace, have observed that the collaboration organisations aim for is frequently indigenous to the informal culture of the workplace, while efforts by management to impose courses to promote 'teamwork' and 'high performance', are resisted (ibid: 1996).

The consultative approach

Gowen's research highlights the pitfalls of non-consultative, 'imposed' education and training. Paul Jurmo discusses the benefits of a participatory approach, where workers are consulted and asked for input into designing, monitoring and evaluating the programme:

> 'Such a perspective on curriculum is particularly relevant to workplace education programmes . . . in high performance workplaces. This is because [it] borrows from the TQM planning process of identifying customer needs, gearing work processes to meet those needs, and continually monitoring and refining those processes.' (Jurmo, 1995:2–3)

The challenge for providers is to see the contradictions in company philosophy and practice, to develop educational provision which is realistic about the positive and negative aspects of these changes. Providers need to encourage learners to explore the contradictions in meaning and practice in their daily work and to develop open dialogue between students, unions and management and work with organisations to ensure better outcomes for learning programmes and for workers. Sarmiento points out the choices of basic skills education in 'high performance' organisations:

> ' . . . workplace literacy programmes can be designed to develop a dispensable, disposable workforce to meet the low literacy and job skill demands . . . . (or be) . . . recognised and handled through the same participatory process and structure that exists in the workplace to identify and solve other kinds of problems.' (Sarmiento, 1991: 2–3)

Training for core and periphery workers

Atkinson provides a model of core and periphery workers which suggests that core workers will be highly trained while the periphery will have only those skills which support ancillary activities and do not require training (Atkinson 1985:28)

With the growing peripheral workforce, entitlement to paid education and training, either in or out of work time has been reduced to a few in the 'core' workforce. When workplace basic skills was developed in the 1980s in most countries provision was in company time. Since the early 1990s this type of provision has been eroded, and this has had a particular affect on opportunities for women, even if they are part of the 'core', to access education and training.

Many of those in the periphery workforce choose this style of working because they have other commitments, such as the need to care for dependents. Years of being unable to enter the core workforce erodes confidence. Mace and Wolfe quote a periphery worker:

> '*Greta, one of our students, talked about how she had taken on her job to 'have time for the kids when they were small.' She went on to say: 'We thought we'd get a real job later on, but you don't. After doing this kind of work, you can't think you're really good for anything else.' (Mace and Wolfe, 1988)*

Training which would extend the skills they have, is not available She recommends paid educational leave:

> '*Making a priority of . . . paid educational leave courses with the emphasis not on remedial training but on 'staff development' can be one way for trade unions and for responsible employers to begin to show some recognition to these essential workers.' (ibid)*

Training is currently not a priority for employers of part time, casual or seasonal workers or for those who are in rural employment or in small business enterprises. These people are all on the periphery of education and training. They need the advocacy of provider organisations and unions to change government and industrial policy.

References

Social science

Aronowitz, S. and DiFazio, W. (1994). *The Jobless Future*. Minneapolis: University of Minnesota Press.

Braverman, H. (1974). *Labour and Monopoly Capital: The Degradation of Work in the Twentieth Century*. London, New York: Monthly Review Press.

Brookfield, S. (1987). *Developing Critical Thinkers: Challenging Adults to explore alternative ways of thinking and acting*. San Francisco: Jossey-Bass.

Brooks, B. (1990). *Working Towards 2000: The Changing Nature of Work*. Sydney: CCH Australia Ltd.

Brown, K. and Hubrich, L. (1995) Framework in Progress. *Learn.* (5) July. Wellington: NZQA

Brown, M. (1994). *Literacies and the Workplace*. Geelong, Victoria: Deakin University.

Burgoyne, J. (1993). The Competency Movement: Issues, Stakeholders and Prospects. *Personnel Review.* 22 (6)

Burns, R. (1995). *The Adult Learner at Work*. Sydney: Business and Professional Publishing.

Burton, L. (1992). *Developing Resourceful Humans: Adult Education Within the Economic Context*. London: Routledge.

Darville, R. (1992). The Economic Push for Literacy: Expansive or Restrictive? In *Proceedings of Adult Literacy: An International Urban Perspective*. New York: UNESCO.

Fontan, J. M. and Shragge, E. (1996). The Chic Resto-Pop: The Reaffirmation of Citizenship Through Socially Useful Work. In Hautecoeur, J. Ed. *Basic Education and Work, Alpha 96* Toronto: UNESCO and Culture Concepts.

Forrester, K., Payne, J. and Ward, K. (1995). *Workplace Learning*. Aldershot: Ashgate Publishing Ltd.

Frank, F. and Hamilton, M. (1993). *Not Just a Number: The Role of Basic Skills Programmes in the Changing Workplace*. Lancaster: Lancaster University.

Gee, J. P. (1994a). *New Alignments and Old Literacies: From Fast Capitalism to the Canon*. Carlton South Victoria: Australian Reading Association.

Gee, J. P. (1994b) Quality, Science and the Lifeworld. *Critical Forum*. Vol.3 (1). Leichhardt: ALBSAC

Gee, J., Hull, G. and Lankshear, C. (1996). *The New Work Order*. St. Leonards: Allen and Unwin.

Gowen, S. G. (1996). How the Reorganisation of Work Destroys Everyday Knowledge. In Hautecoeur. Ed. *Basic Education and Work: Alpha 96*. Toronto: UNESCO and Cuture Concepts.

Hughes, K. (1995). Really Useful Knowledge. In Mayo, M and Thompson, J. Eds. *Adult Learning, Critical Intelligence and Social Change* Leicester: NIACE.

Lankshear, C. (1994). Self Direction and Empowerment: Critical Language Awareness and the 'New Work Order.' In O'Connor, P. Ed. *Thinking Work*. Sydney: ALBSAC.

Levett, A. and Lankshear, C. (1994). Literacies, Workplaces and the Demands of New Times. In Brown, M. Ed., *Literacies and the Workplace: A collection of Original Essays*. Geelong: Deakin University Press.

Mace, J. and Wolfe, M. (1988). Women, Work and Release. *Adult Education*, 61(1)

Marsick, V.J. Ed. *Learning in the Workplace*. Beckenham, Kent: Croom Helm.

O'Connor, P. (1993). Crossing the Borders of Workers' Literacy. *Focus: Adult Literacy and Basic Skills Action Coalition*, 3. Leichhardt: ALBSAC.

O'Connor, P. (1994). *Thinking Work*. Sydney: ALBSAC.

Pollert, A. (1987). *The Flexible Firm: A Model in Search of a Reality*. Warwick Papers in Industrial Relations (19) Coventry: Warwick University.

Probert, B. and Wajcman, J. (1988). Technological Change and the Future of Work. In *Journal of Industrial Relations*. (September) Sydney:Industrial Relations Society of Australia.

Schultz, K. (1992). *Training for Basic Skills or Educating Workers? Changing Conceptions of Workplace Literacy Programs*. Berkeley: National Centre for Research in Vocational Education.

Toms, J. (1995). Competency-Based Training: Methodology or Ideology? A Critical Approach. *Critical Forum*. 4, 2. Leichhardt: ALBSAC.

Management texts
Boyett, J. H. and Conn, H. P. (1992). *Workplace 2000: The Revolution Reshaping American Business* . New York: Plume, Penguin.
Collard, R. (1993). *Total Quality Success Through People*. London: Institute of Personnel Management.
Drucker, P. F. (1993). *Post-Capitalist Society*. New York: Harper.
Eurich, N. (1985). *Corporate Classrooms. The Learning Business*. Princeton: Carnegie Foundation for the Advancement of Teaching.
Kumazawa, M. and Yamada, J. (1989). Jobs and Skills under the Lifelong Nenko Employment Practice. *The Transformation of Work* London: Unwin Hyman.
Omega. (1989). *Literacy in the Workplace: The Executive Perspective*. Bryn Mawr: Omega Group.
Peters, T. (1992). *Liberation Management: Necessary Disorganisation for the Nanosecond Nineties*. New York: Fawcett.
Peters, T. (1994). *Crazy Times Call for Crazy Organisations*. New York: Vintage Books.
Senge, P. (1990). *The Fifth Discipline: The Art and Practice of the Learning Organisation* . New York: Doubleday.
Wiggenhorn, W. (1990). Motorola U: When Training Becomes Education. *Harvard Business Review*, (July-August)
Young, C. (1992). Workplace Reform: So Much To Gain. *NZ Business*. Auckland: NZ Business Journal.

Research/reports
Atkinson, J. (1985). Flexibility: Planning for an Uncertain Future. *Manpower Policy and Practice: The IMS Review* Brighton: IMS.
Atkinson, J. (188). Recent Changes in the Internal Labour Market Structure in the UK. In Buitelaar, W. Ed. *Technology at Work: Labour Studies in England, Germany and the Netherlands* Aldershot: Averbury Ashgate Publishing Ltd.
Bailey, T. (1990). *Changes in the Nature and Structure of Work: Implications for Skill Requirements and Skills Formation*. Berkeley: National Centre for Research in Vocational Education.
Carnevale, A. P., Gainer, L. J. and Meltzer, A. S. (1990). *Workplace Basics: The Skills Employers Want* . Washington DC: US Department of Labor, American Society for Training and Development.
McGivney, V. (1994). *Wasted Potential: Training and Career Progression for Part-Time and Temporary Workers*. Leicester: NIACE.
Tuckett, A. (1991). *Towards a Learning Workforce*. Leicester: NIACE.

Policy documents
Brown, K. and Hubrich, L. (1995). Framework in Progress. *Learn*, 5 (July) Wellington: NZQA
Confederation of British Industry. (1989). *Towards a Skills Revolution*. London: CBI.
Drouin, M. J. (1990). *Workforce Literacy: An Economic Challenge for Canada* . Montreal: Hudson Institute.
Harman, D. and Lerche, R. (1988). *The Bottom Line: Basic Skills in the Workplace*. New York: US Department of Education. US Department of Labor.
New Zealand Qualifications Authority. (1993). *Qualifications 21st Century*. 'Quality' Conference Papers. Wellington: Victoria University and NZQA.

Unions

Cornfield, D. (1987). *Workers, Managers, and Technological Change*. New York: Plenum Press.

Nygaard, K. (1980). *The Computer in the Workplace: Lessons From the Norwegian Experience*. Wellington: Industrial Relations Centre. Victoria University.

Parker M. and Slaughter, J. (1994). Working Smart: A Union Guide to Participation Programmes and Reengineering / With Union Strategy Guide. *Labor Notes* (Nov.)

Rainbird, H. (1990). *Training Matters*. Warwick: Basil Blackwell Ltd.

Sarmiento, T. (1991). Do Workplace Literacy Programs Promote High Skills or Low Wages? Suggestion for Future Evaluations of Workplace Literacy Programs. *National Governors' Association Labor Notes*. 64 (7–11 July). Columbia: Centre for Policy Research, National Governors' Association.

Practice and guidelines

Jurmo, P. (1995). Curriculum: Creating Multiple Learning Opportunities. *Technical Notes* New York: New York State Education Department Workplace Education Project.

Wilkinson, S. (1994). *Quality and Workplace Education: A Guide for Practitioners*. Edinburgh: Scottish Community Education Council.

The learning organisation

Competency-based training (CBT)

A presentation of perspectives on competency-based training must necessarily open with an inquiry into the origins and rationale for the movement. Advocates and critics speak to the issue, and questions are asked about whether competency amounts to a proper acknowledgement of skills or a means of gatekeeping. Finally, through the texts, the hidden functions of competencies are explored.

The colonisation of education

During the 1960s and 1970s, schools and adult education providers focussed on the development of thinking process, i.e. the ability to make comparisons, consider alternatives, etc. The more progressive and radical educators were engaged in programmes which enabled learners to critique their world, pose as well as solve problems.

Industry and other agencies concerned with control have demanded a 'back to basics', a return to authoritarian forms of education. Since the early 1980s, that battle has begun to be won, manifested in part in the competency movement. Burgoyne asks

> ' . . . whether the competency movement represents an attempt to realign the education system away from one of its traditional functions of producing citizens who can critically question and help reformulate the existing social and political order..[or] produces people who are skilled at implementing the current order without questioning it . . .' (Burgoyne, 1992:3)

Forrester *et al* (1995), Collins (1989), O'Connor (1994) and others have perceived a colonisation of the workplace by business, a successful take-over of the decisions about what counts as knowledge and skills and the measurement of achievement. From 1987 in Australia:

> 'Education witnessed a call for competency based vocational education based on the premise that skill development would improve economic growth, reduce unemployment and hone Australia's international market competitiveness.' (Toms, 1995:62)

The same phenomenon was occurring in the US, UK, Canada and New Zealand in vocational and non-vocational spheres.

The role of competencies

Charles Woodruffe defines competencies thus:

> ' . . . one of the sets of behaviour that the person must display in order to perform the tasks and functions of a job with competence' (Woodruffe, 1991:31)

Competencies have been adopted in industrialised countries over the last decade as a means of measuring performance of knowledge and skills.

Learners receive recognition for discrete units of learning towards regional or national certificates which are largely determined by industry, through training organisations, based on industry needs. Industry works with the qualifications authority to place competencies at the appropriate level of the country's national qualifications framework (UK, NZ), or industry/ enterprise standards framework (Australia), or their Canadian and American counterparts.

Thus, according to the literature, competency-based training (CBT) has been successfully established internationally by alliances between bureaucrats, unions, and large established business (see, for instance, Foyster 1990).

Advocacy and criticism

Today, the stated benefits of competency-based education in free market economies include that: students can master competencies at their own pace; that standards can be held constant; that they encourage greater account- ability of learners and instructors; they give recognition to previously uncertificated skills; mastery can continue throughout a lifetime in any number of different institutions (and is therefore more flexible than previous systems of learning); and they are matched to performance (more easily measured). (See, for instance, Field, 1990.)

Providers have noted that in many instances low paid manual staff have been included in their organisation's training agenda for the first time. Competencies, claim their designers, work equally well for vocational and non-vocational skills and knowledge. For instance:

> 'Good curriculum design for teaching reading is competency based or performance based. This means that the design includes clearly defined learning objectives for each reading process to be taught and corresponding instructional activities leading to measurable mastery of those objectives.' (Carnevale et al, 1990:78)

Debate over CBT is fierce. Foyster persuades:

> ' . . . why adopt competency-based training? Because those who have adopted it have found that CBT produces more skilled, more satisfied workers, more quickly.' (Foyster, 1990:2)

He adds:

> '*CBT requires more planning and management than traditional education . . . it is spreading, despite this 'handicap' of additional planning, because it usually works much more effectively to bring employees to the required skill levels than do traditional methods.*' (ibid: 2)

However, more serious limitations are acknowledged even by advocates of the approach. Laurie Field, vocational trainer and author in Sydney Australia points out that competency based training tends to:

> '*focus very much on the current job (and thus downplay the need for broad based skills or the ability to work with new technology); assume that once someone is competent, he or she stays competent; overemphasise areas which can be divided into self contained, observable tasks, and ignore areas such as pride in one's work and craftsmanship.*' (Field, 1990:77)

Some enthusiasts of competency based training find the attempts to implement policy frustrating:

> ' . . . *practical implementation is proving more difficult than most organisations, policy makers and experts were expecting . . . so far, . . . successful implementation . . . has been rare . . .*' (Lloyd and Cook, 1993)

A search of the literature reveals a great deal more criticism than advocacy. Strongly critical of the competency movement, Toms argues that the meaning of the word 'competence' is elusive, and that it is a

> '*one-dimensional categorisation of tasks that form the basis of a systematised curriculum.*' (Toms, 1995:47).

He adds that competencies allow only one correct form of understanding. Burgoyne examines the economic argument for competencies, that the lack of a 'common currency' for occupational standards and qualifications, leads to inefficiencies in the market (Burgoyne, 1992:8). Toms comments that competencies have been sold

> '*as a form of skills currency to obtain higher wages.*' (Toms, 1995:55)

Behaviourist and Taylorist overtones

The alignment of competency based training to Behaviourism and Taylorism is explored by a number of other critics. Velde and Svensson note the prevalence of the behavioural model, particularly in the UK and Australia and cite Jones and Moore, who suggest that

> ' . . . *those features that constitute its virtues from a policy point of view (the clear and simple operationalisation of deaggregated 'skills' and measurable standards of performance) . . . condemn it theoretically and methodologically.*' (Velde and Svensson, 1996:2)

Brown (1994) notes how competencies are Taylorist in that they rely entirely on the observable inference of outcomes (performance) in a controlled environment, and believes their central role is to provide an objective that can be readily defined and measured. Burns, a psychologist with the Australian Department of Education and Employment Training (DEET), strongly criticises the behaviourist objectives which, he says,

> '. . impose a 'top down' approach to designing a learning system in which skill development and the educational achievement of the learners are subordinate to job performance objectives and the needs of the economy. In this context, learning becomes a tool of corporate balance sheets and political decisions . . . Humanist values do not enter the equation.' (Burns, 1995:42)

Lankshear claims that this approach is a powerful initiation into passivity and political impotence, and amounts to 'donating' competencies to passive recipients who learn how to understand and to follow. (Lankshear and Lawler, 1987)

Others anxious about its 'Taylorist' overtones, claim that it constitutes (with its roots in behavioural psychology):

> 'an extreme form of reductionism which attempts to explain complex phenomena by discrete, standardised concepts. Competency based education has its roots in behavioural psychology and champions the methods of behaviourism.' (Jarvis and Prais, 1989)

Forrester *et al* agree that competency based training is behaviourist, functionalist and at odds with a post–Fordist world. It is said to be progressive in that it captures learning outcomes better, but a preoccupation with complexities excludes debate about values and purposes. (Forrester *et al*, 1995:138–139)

More than competence

Saunders is concerned with the inability of the competency model to address all the components of skill and knowledge. He points out that competencies cannot measure all the skills that contribute to success in the workplace, noting the difficulties, under this system, of taking into account underpinning knowledge, personal skills and qualities, as well as the management of factors specific to the workplace (eg. interactional culture).

Saunders advocates an extension of the notion of competence to a broader concept of 'capability.' He also observes that competence is uneasily placed between training and qualifying.

> 'There is no sense in a system which simply leaves the working population with the skills they already have, even if they are now able to produce a certificate to show that this is the case.' (Saunders, 1995b: Prob.6)

Canadian Professor Nancy Jackson agrees that competencies are an inadequate measurement, where skill is said to equal competence, and argues strongly that skills are much more complex, depending on other factors such as the sociopolitical context in which an skill (or knowledge) is demonstrated (Jackson, 1993b). Toms explains:

> 'Anyone who has worked knows there is far more to being successful in a job than carrying out the basic tasks competently. Jobs are seldom performed in isolation.' (Toms, 1995:61, quoting Jessup, 1991:36)

This view would seem to be supported by Peter Senge, writing about the 'learning organisation', and highly regarded by 'high performance' organisations. He comments:

> '. . we are taught to break apart problems, to fragment the world . . . but we pay a hidden, enormous price. We can no longer see the consequences of our actions; we lose our intrinsic sense of connection to a larger whole.' (Senge, 1990:1)

Wright, in an article about learning in the public service, agrees that survival in the workplace is not just about competencies but also about 'socialisation and the establishment of one's own identity in the workplace.' (Wright, 1994: 56)

Mayo and Thompson compare current narrow educational objectives with more holistic objectives of earlier decades. They record the reaction to lively educational debate of the 1970s, and the change in the 1980s where adult education was driven into 'safer' channels. They note that the language of credits and transfers and progression has replaced a content and purpose that once addressed the needs of the 'whole person'. (Mayo and Thompson, 1995)

Jackson asks 'why and for whom competency measures continue to appear as an intelligent and rational choice' (Jackson, 1993b:47) She argues:

> ' . . . that competency based curriculum measures need to be understood primarily as a tool of administrative rather than instructional reform. That is, they provide a means of setting educational objectives and organising programme delivery that promises 'efficiency', 'effectiveness' and 'responsiveness' to the needs of industry; all this in a political climate where these goals have come to be seen as the essence of good management practice in educational institutions.' (ibid:47)

Skills acknowledgement or gatekeeping?

Jackson (1993a), O'Connor (1994), and Cooper (1992) observe the credentialing aspects of CBT, where entry qualifications are imposed which did not previously exist.

> 'The focus on narrow or isolated conceptions . . . . .will have the effect of spreading credentialism and paper qualifications to industries and/or occupations where they were previously not required.' (O'Connor, 1994:18–19)

This view is supported by Burgoyne, who also discusses how, in terms of competency, people are presented by human resource personnel as manageable commodities rather than self willed agents. (Burgoyne, 1993:6)

The deskilling of educators

Some critics have noted the effect that competencies have had on deskilling educators. Collins emphasises its 'controlling and restructuring influence' in a collection of readings related to CBT published by Deakin University, Australia:

> 'the competency movement defines knowledge in the light of bureaucratic and corporate needs . . . resulting in reductionist competence statements . . . [which] deskill the educator's role . . .' (Collins, 1983)

Toms, too, comments on the hegemonic and disenfranchising impact that the competency movement is having on educators, thereby stifling debate:

> 'Competency technology is . . . being used to manipulate the training agenda by governments, unions and industry . . . Educators have been captured by the ideology . . .' (Toms, 1995:63)

He adds:

> '. . the silences surrounding the sociopolitical in the CBT rhetoric are deafening.' (ibid:51)

The economic imperative

Jackson notes that the one-dimensional view contained in CBT ' . . . obscures the politics of skill and the terrain of struggle of workers to retain power . . .' She observes:

> 'teachers are no longer the official source of decisions about either the ends or the means of the instructional process. Their role instead becomes a 'support function', as facilitators of objectives and implementors of instructional models determined by others . . . .' (Jackson, 1993b:50)

She continues:

> 'In fact, upon closer examination it is very clear who is actually leading CBE/T initiatives in the US, Canada, Great Britain and Australia. All are effectively driven by governments, or, as John Field . . . put it so nicely, 'selective coalitions between (parts of) capital and (parts of) the state.' . . . . . Governments, whether pro-labour or pro-business, are pushing CBE/T precisely because it provides them the means to present an appearance of serving the needs of industry at a time when their political survival depends on them doing so.' (ibid:54)

Burgoyne notes with interest that the 'scientific' basis of the competency movement is so far behind and detached from the current wisdom of the social sciences. He suggests that the explanation is probably political, and warns of the
danger that the bureaucracy of the competency movement may actually inhibit
enterprise. (Burgoyne, 1993)

Progression and promotion

Warnings that by the year 2000 there will not be enough qualified people for
jobs are common. Texts describe a two-tiered society (those who can access
jobs and promotional opportunities and those who can't because they are
unemployable in the new work order) by the year 2000 unless training is
implemented.

Skills enabling progression

Jorie W. Phillipi uses examples from the military in advocating training. She
describes people with literacy skills of between a fourth to eighth grade level
as 'intermediate literates' on whom training should be focussed.
Unemployment is seen as directly relating to a skills lack.

> 'What is needed to solve the growing employment problem . . . is instruction in
> on-the-job reading skills through programs to qualify unemployed 'intermediate
> literates' for the job market. (Phillipi, 1988:659)

Declining internal promotion opportunities

In the workplace, prior to the 1980s, moving up a job ladder within firms was
an important route to stable employment. Bailey, in his article 'Changes in
the Nature and Structure of Work' (Bailey, 1990:34–39) , explains that now
firms are trying to move away from training for upgrading (internal promotion). Now there are more ports of entry, increasingly based on educational
credentials, and a consequent reduction of opportunities for those with low
qualifications.

Are qualifications the answer?

Marie Jose Drouin discusses human capital and screening theory (where
training on the job creates credentials about a worker's trainability and
influencing chances of promotion) and structural unemployment. She points
out the responsibility of industry to train, rather than 'buy' qualified workers,
and concludes that workers will

> ' . . . need to improve basic or enabling skills to facilitate adaptability and adjust-
> ment to job turnover and job redefinition.' (Drouin, 1990:18)

Statistics are quoted to promote the positive effects of workplace training:

> *'Available data tend to support the fact that on-the-job learning – especially formal learning – can increase one's earnings by as much as 30%.' (Carnevale et al, 1990:12)*

However, this view has been challenged in the literature. Ken Levine argues that wide possession of a particular literacy competence is not what is desired by those in control of employment, since this will devalue it. He quotes Hirsch (1977), who describes literacy and education in general, as belonging to what he calls the 'positional economy.' Not only is it more valuable when less widely available, but when more people achieve skills qualifications the qualification requirements increase. He uses Hirsch's (1977) analogy:

> *'. . once some people stand on tiptoe in order to get a better view, others will be forced to do the same, everyone ending up in their original, relative positions.' (Hirsch, in Levine, 1982:259)*

Burns notes that a narrow perception of education

> *'leads to a dangerous assumption that current unemployment is due to lack of relevant skills and that once this situation is improved, jobs will be there . . . a training led recovery is very unlikely.' (Burns, 1995:43)*

Other critics show how some rising educational requirements are not necessary for level of skills required for occupational tasks, that they simply act as gatekeepers. Glynda Hull's and Sheryl Gowen's ethnographic research illustrates how education policy and workplace practices keep people in entry level jobs. (See Gowen, 1992 and Hull, 1992.)

Glynda Hull (1994) discusses the 'Literacy Myth', that Literacy provision will equal job advancement, increase choice. It includes, she says, a belief in the deficit model, and power of functional literacy tuition to economically improve business operations and worker's prospects. She also looks at the flip side, where 'illiteracy' is used to justify low pay and lack of promotional prospects.

Sheryl Gowen (1992) looks at the ways in which educational policies and workplace structures contribute to workers remaining in entry level jobs for a lifetime. She shows how workers' real competencies are unrecognised, ignored or masked by workplace organisational structures and processes.

Others add that despite the implications and claims to the contrary, equipping adults with rudimentary literacy will probably have a negligible capacity, in itself, to combat low pay, unemployment or general social deprivation (see Levine, 1982 and Sarmiento, 1991). Gee contends that although education may predict initial salary and job title, it does not predict promotion or productivity. (Gee, 1994a)

Promotional prospects are dimmer for those on the periphery. In her report of a research project undertaken by the UK National Institute for Adult and Continuing Education to investigate training provision for this group, Veronica McGivney states:

> '. . part-time workers are at a distinct disadvantage regarding promotion and career progression, whatever the occupation or level of work.' (McGivney, 1994:17)

Banking and liberating education

The literature thus far has described and illustrated a decline in education as a democratising force. Concurrently, the concept of *functional literacy* has emerged as a way of describing the degree of literacy necessary to cope with the demands of society and the workplace. This final chapter will examine the literature promoting a functional approach, its links to economic development and to the competence movement, and its role in obscuring and legitimising current exploitative work practices. Ways in which tutors may unwittingly collaborate in providing a very restricted curriculum and delivery are noted. The chapter will also present the works of writers who advocate a more democratic, participatory and collaborative approach, and of critical theorists outlining a liberatory approach.

The pervading concept of functional literacy has been denounced by critical theorists of the 'new literacy studies' as 'banking' education, 'improper' or 'autonomous' literacy. All of these terms describe a restricted, domesticating and dehumanising form of literacy, contrasting strongly with more liberating, 'proper' and critical perspectives. (See Freire, 1972; Lankshear and Lawler, 1987; Street, 1984.)

Links to economic development

Levine discusses how 'functional' literacy has achieved

> 'an unchallenged domination over an important sphere of human activity' (Levine, 1982: 249)

and claims it has come to have 'an extreme elasticity of meaning' (*ibid*). He subjects the 'jumble of ad hoc and largely mistaken assumptions about literacy's economic, social and political dimensions' (*ibid*) to careful scutiny, and attempts to reconstruct the process by which functional literacy became synonymous with work.

Levine traces the development of 'functionality' in relation to literacy through UNESCO documentation since 1947, notes the changes in thinking from humanistic (where literacy was seen as a basic human right) through the development of grade equivalences, to the Experimental World Literacy Programme (EWLP), established in 1964, which

> 'very strongly emphasised the economic and development potential of literacy.' (ibid:254)

Levine explains that this link came about because of the failure of programmes, whatever the rationale, to meet desired goals.

> *'After the disppointments and failures of previous efforts, the new thinking regarding literacy – adult, selective, developmental, participative – required a label that suggested the economic benefits that could be expected from investment in literacy.' (ibid:254)*

Functionality was taken up the 'Right to Read' campaigns in the late 1960s and early 1970s in the US and UK. Brian Street (1984) comments that by this time:

> *'the conception of 'functional' literacy [had] underpinned development and literacy programmes across the world . . .' (Street, 1984:183)*

The EWLP pilot schemes were now all linked to training in technological skills. Street comments:

> *' . . . the ultimate determination of the programme lay with financial and commercial interests, with governments acting simply as mediators and as providers of the 'risk capital' in terms of the infrastructure of education and training. The subjects themselves were a form of 'plant' whose effectiveness could be maximised by the employment of new 'educational technology' in the form of 'literacy skills' thereby enabling greater surplus to be extracted from them.' (Street, 1984:184)*

In 1978, UNESCO had altered their perspective:

> *'The possession of skills perceived as necessary by particular persons and groups to fulfil their own self-determined objectives as family and community members, citizens, consumers, job-holders, and members of social, religious or other associations of their choosing. This includes the ability to obtain information they want and to use that information for their own and others' well-being; the ability to read and write adequately to satisfy the requirements they set for themselves as being important for their own lives; the ability to deal positively with demands made on them by society; and the ability to solve the problems they face in their daily lives.' (UNESCO, 1978)*

Yet the earlier, more limited view continues to be at the base of many authoritative publications and is particularly heavily promoted in US government policy documents. Technical competence in reading and writing came to be the measure in national literacy surveys also. Research reports, revealing low levels of functional literacy in society (eg. Wickert, 1989) and in the workplace (Diehl and Mikulecky, 1980) add further weight to the need to focus on technical competence.

The limitations of a technical kind of competence

Much technical competence involves understanding, reading, following and reproducing. Tom Sticht, when describing the reading skills a functionally literate person might have in relation to work, focusses particularly on reading tasks imposed by an external agent.

Levine notices how the United States National Research Centre and Sticht . . .

> 'heavily emphasise reading skills in attempting to characterise the minimum level of socially useful competence'. (Levine, 1982:261)

Levine is concerned at the way writing seems to be ignored:

> 'Writing, in all but its most rudimentary forms, is omitted from existing conceptions and operationalisations of functional literacy. Yet it is, on the whole, writing competencies that are capable of initiating change.' (ibid:262)

Altered consciousness

Levine, again, notes that functional literacy goals continue to fail to be achieved. He asserts that:

> 'current notions of functional literacy . . . obscure . . . identification of proper targets, goals and standards of achievement . . . by promising, though failing to produce, a quantitively precise, unitary standard of 'survival' literacy . . . (they) . . . encourage the idea that relatively low levels of literacy will . . . result in . . . universally desired outcomes . . . employment . . . economic growth . . . job advancement . . . social integration.' (Levine, 1982:250)

Brian Street notices how writers and practitioners currently in the field sometimes get caught up in recommending and offering a more restricted, functional, autonomous form of literacy. The 'autonomous' model, focusing on functional competence in technical skills, is seen by Street as legitimising inequalities in society. Aware of the affect of 'improper' or 'autonomous' literacy in keeping people *un*conscious, Street observes that it is supposedly technical and neutral . . .

> ' . . . (but) . . . some forms of literacy programme actually impair criticalness and . . . what is being imparted is not a technical skill but an ideology.' (Street, 1984:186)

Henry Giroux agrees. In his introduction to Freire's *Literacy: Reading the Word and the World*, he refers to Antonio Gramsci, whose notion of literacy suggests . . .

> 'that it may have less to do with the task of teaching people how to read and write than with producing and legitimating oppressive and exploitative social practices.' (Freire and Macedo, 1987:Introduction)

Giroux adds:

> 'In the United States, the language of literacy is almost exclusively linked to popular forms of liberal and right wing discourse that reduce it to either a functional

perspective tied to narrowly conceived economic interests or to an ideology designed to initiate the poor, the underprivileged, and minorities into the logic of a unitary, dominant cultural tradition.' (ibid)

In his 1985 analysis of the conservative, liberal and radical debate over schooling he explains that employers want an education system closely tuned to the job market, and how the concept of 'excellence' has been redefined as basic skills, technical training, and classroom discipline. (*Aronowitz and Giroux, 1985*)

Street observes the exclusion of critical literacy from employer-led education and training. Education systems, he says, traditionally decide on, and develop 'intellectual competence'. However:

'. . if 'intellectual competence' includes, for instance, critical consciousness, then it might well be in conflict with productivity (in the workplace).' (Street, 1984:185)

Street claims that to be logical and literate in the sense described here, is to be schooled to accept the hegemony of the ruling class. He advocates literacy work understood as social practice, which develops consciousness and criticism of ideology. (Street, 1984:183–212)

Tutor collaboration

Ian Falk examines the relationship between collaborative negotiation and power by analysing classroom conversations. Through a transcription of a classroom Adult Community Education lesson, he shows how 'negotiated' classroom practice can yet serve to maintain power and control over the student group. In this case, it amounted to:

' . . . jointly reconstructing an acceptance of the teacher's pre-selected activities,' (Falk, 1994: 231)

thereby maintaining the status quo where the people in power decide what learning has value.

Sheryl Gowen notes a shift in which instructors have now a support role in interpreting, facilitating objectives, and delivering predetermined competencies. She notes also a broader shift in the domain of needs, from learner to employer. (Gowen, 1996) More democratic workplaces, more empowered workers, and a broader view of literacy (enabling workers to participate in programme goals and curriculum development), are thus denied.

Zacharias-Jutz agrees that the functional approach to workplace literacy does not address a number of critical issues such as worker participation in programme planning, nor provide for a proper balance between industry and worker needs, and calls for a more worker-centered perspective. (Zacharias-Jutz, 1993:91–105)

Paul Jurmo quotes Susan Imel and Sandra Kerka (1992), who review the early purposes of employee basic skills programmes and believe that a more worker centred perspective can empower workers to affect changes in their workplace:

> 'Since the mid-1980s, workplace education tended to be seen as a means of helping employees perform particular 'high priority job tasks as determined by management.' More recently, however, some in the field have conceived of programmes as a means of changing not just 'the behaviour of individual employees but the larger work organisation as well.'(Jurmo, 1994:3)

Jurmo claims that the former perspective represents the functional context approach while the latter perspective is a more 'collaborative' approach.

A liberatory approach

To Lankshear, functional literacy 'resembles the act of rearranging the deck chairs on the *Titanic*.' (Lankshear, 1993:216–218)

In his earlier work, with Moira Lawler, he presents domesticating (functional) literacy as *dys*functional and 'improper', and liberating literacy as functional and 'proper'. He compares this domesticating function, with the role literacy played in the emergence of a working class consciousness between 1790 and 1832. He states:

> ' . . . the pursuit, attainment, and practice of proper forms of literacy was a vital galvanising element within the active role played by working folk in making themselves a class.' (Lankshear and Lawler, 1987:81)

The Australian Department of Education and Employment's view of literacy is enlightened when compared to its counterparts in America and Britain, in that it includes more than reading and writing and acknowledges a critical element:

> 'Literacy is the ability to read and use written information and to write appropriately, in a range of contexts. It is used to develop knowledge and understanding, to achieve personal growth and to function effectively in our society. Literacy also includes the recognition of numbers and basic mathematical signs and symbols within text . . . involves the integration of speaking, listening and critical thinking with reading and writing. Effective literacy is intrinsically purposeful, flexible and dynamic and continues to develop throughout an individual's lifetime. (DEET, 1991)

Paulo Freire regards being able to read the 'word' as synonymous with being able to read the 'world', i.e. that literacy is a social justice issue, where to become literate is to be able to reflect on, and act in society for change. (see Freire and Macedo, 1987) Others, such as Lankshear and Lawler,1987; Ooijens, 1994 and Street, 1984 take a similar position. Freire says of the functional approach:

> ' . . . he who thinks the working class is uncultured and incompetent, and thus needs to be liberated from top to bottom – this type of educator does not really

have anything to do with freedom or democracy.' (Freire and Macedo, 1987: 40)

He advises:

' . . . *knowledge is not a piece of data, something immobilized, concluded, finished, something to be transferred by one who acquired it to one who still does not possess it . . . ' (ibid:41)*

and, further:

'It is not viable to separate literacy from the productive processes of society. The ideal is a concomitant approach in which literacy evolves in various environments, such as the workplace.' (ibid:50)

Education, says Freire, is political, and this must be acknowledged in the proper development of literacy in any context. The process of becoming literate is the process of coming to understand how the dominant culture decides what counts as knowledge, thereby devaluing the knowledge of subordinate cultures and creating the conditions for their failure. (*ibid*, 1987)

Literacy and blue collar workers

Stephen Brookfield, writing about developing critical thinking, notices the inconsistencies of management and human resource talk in which encourage- ment is given for critical thinking by white and blue collar workers, and yet front line workers are denied specific training in the development of a critical consciousness. (Brookfield, 1987:144–151)

He records there are greater limits placed on the expression of critical thinking by blue collar workers. This, says Brookfield, is counter-productive for management. He draws on the findings of management consultant Tom Peters in which critical thinking is an indicator of excellence in his study of ten top American corporations:

'It is clear . . . that workplaces in which innovation, creativity and flexibility are evident are workplaces in which critical thinkers are prized . . . [and where] . . . leaps of imagination that take companies beyond currently accepted modes of production are more likely to take place. Critical thinking, then, can be seen as the central element in improving organisational performance.' (Brookfield, 1987:139)

Some implications for provision

Implications for provision that can be drawn from the literature on competen- cies and how they relate to a banking or liberatory kind of education, progres- sion and promotion are far-ranging. The issues are highly politically charged, and the actions workplaces and providers take, depend both on their world view and their willingness to risk standing outside current 'wisdom.'

Banking and making money

A discussion of the implications of this chapter must examine the distinction between education and training. Boxall distinguishes them thus:

> 'Education comprises all those learning experiences which improve an individual's general knowledge and overall competence. It is person orientated rather than job orientated . . . Training consists of all those learning activities which improve an individual's performance on a particular job. It is specific rather than general.' (Boxall, 1995:154)

Wringe offers a stronger distinction:

> 'training . . . 'the production of a conforming mind' and education . . . 'the development of a rational autonomy.' (quoted in Prince, 1992:65)

When we talk about competencies, we are talking about training, or a 'banking' kind of education. This is certainly far behind current wisdom about good education practice, yet teachers comply, possibly because of a lack of educational debate and support. Gowen is troubled by:

> 'the way that literacy educators can be co-opted into extending the undercutting of worker knowledge by focussing on 'functional context' workplace literacy programmes' (Gowen, 1996)

Such approaches, she claims,

> 'will probably ensure profitable consulting work, but do little for those on the bottom . . .' (ibid)

Providers of literacy in the workplace are in danger of opting for profitable consultancy work where industry has determined 'proper' objectives, at the expense of good practice which is the result of thorough educational research and vigorous debate.

What we already know

A common practice in literacy education in the workplace, is to prepare a training needs analysis from which a programme of learning can be designed. Decisions tend to be made primarily by education specialists and managers, prior to instruction, and emphasise the breaking down of jobs into tasks and skills. (Jurmo, 1994:7) The functional context approach relies heavily on this method. However, as Schultz points out:

> 'What is striking about literacy audits is that they almost always lead to lists of skills and subskills rather than to a broader understanding of teaching and learning literate practices . . . the dominant ideology which supports this single way of conceptualising the curriculum necessarily limits the possibilities for teaching and

learning in these programmes . . . (it is) . . . essentially Tayloristic . . . based on breaking work into its smallest and most basic elements and defining jobs narrowly so that they are relatively easy to learn.' (Schultz, 1992:V)

A better educational model is participatory education, effectively used by literacy workers in the developed and third world to advance people's ability to 'read the word and the world'. The model is explained for the context of education in the workplace by Paul Jurmo:

'Curriculum should be viewed not as a 'set of workbooks' but as the process through which educators, learners, and other stakeholders continually (1) identify learning objectives, and (2) plan, implement, refine, and expand on a variety of activities to meet those objectives.' (Jurmo, 1995:2)

Such a model is sharply at odds with competency based education, where there is little room for learner participation in the refinement of objectives. Paul Jurmo reasserts what has been known by educators for decades:

'Workers . . . need to be involved in setting learning goals. If they don't see an education program as relevant to their interests, they are unlikely to participate actively.' (Jurmo, 1994:5)

He advocates integrated learning, focussing on transferable skills, which learners are actively involved in developing. Clearly the CBT paradigm does not fit here, and providers will need to consider how much their own educational understandings are being compromised in the implementation of narrow, performance based programmes where students have minimal developmental input. It may be possible to point out to employers and participants, from some analysis of workplace practices, gaps between employees actual experience and the competency description. This awareness could be used to broaden the course content.

Integration is a key concern, also, of Laurie Field and Denis Drysdale, authors of a handbook developed for trainers in Australia and rewritten for the UK market. Although they are more conservative in their approach, they observe the increasingly blurred boundaries between technologies and jobs and recognise the necessity of providing integrated training to meet these changes. They make the following qualification:

'This does not mean that specialist skill formation programmes need to be watered down, but there is an increasing demand for generalists who are familiar with a range of systems and their interconnections. A challenge for trainers . . . will be to develop training modules that reflect these cross disciplinary connections.' (Field and Drysdale, 1991:61)

Wider knowledge

A major difficulty with CBT, noted in the literature, is its inability to address learning that is not able to be proven by performance, and observed. Providers of education who use this system are dissuaded from requiring research, comparison and analysis of different presentations of knowledge, because this process, and the knowledge gained, cannot easily be measured, assessed and certificated. Integrated learning is also difficult to measure.

In many workplaces conception of a task generally remains at management level; there is only one 'right way', and workers are expected to do no more than follow instructions. The CBT practice of measuring learning bites is comfortable in this environment.

Providers who reflect this practice in their programmes are not only giving their students a second rate education, but are also doing a disservice to organisations they work with who are genuinely interested in democratic, participative workplaces. At the very least, the critical literature implies that programmes need to offer more than competencies.

Credentialism

A number of authors have discussed the weaknesses of CBT. One such weakness is 'credentialism', where qualifications are now necessary where none were previously, and people have to prove they can do something in order to get the piece of paper they need for promotion, or, more often, to keep their own job.

This suggests that, so not to end up teaching what students already know, providers need to assess individuals' skill levels, ensure that the student gains recognition for prior learning, and teach on an individual basis other necessary skills.

This presents several practical and ethical problems for providers: the time and cost for workers in gaining recognition for prior learning, the waste of 'teaching' what 'students' already know but need qualifications for, the cost and educational value of individual *vs* group learning.

Corporate control of teaching decisions

In the 1960s and 1970s, teachers were generally entrusted to make informed and professional decisions about the learning needs of their students, how to develop a suitable learning environment, and how to assess understandings as well as skills. Under CBT, these professional skills are redundant. Jackson quotes Moore, 1987:

> ' . . . learning becomes the province of corporate, non educational interests.'
> (Jackson, 1993b:50)

Indeed, many teachers no longer feel confident about their ability to assess learning that is independent of ranges, elements and performance criteria. Cumbersome moderation and verification processes decrease professional autonomy and increase workloads.

The literature points to a crisis of confidence, led by employers, in the capabilities of educators to deliver. It is urgent that educators debate the values and purposes of CBT, to consider its effect on students and teachers as professional workers.

Teacher training

Freire warns that in engaging in this banking kind of education, a radical teacher can make the mistake of using teaching methods that support the system she would want to challenge. (Freire and Macedo, 1987)

New generations of teachers (and company trainers) need exposure to a broad range of educational theory. Falk urges that teacher training and professional development should include critical discourse and language analysis [i.e. that the gap between theory and practice should be bridged]. (Falk, 1994:230)

Modelling critical thinking

Providers of education need to be able to understand and to model critical thinking strategies in order to enhance these skills in learners. With critical thinking, Brookfield explains:

> ' . . . . workers identify, question, and change the assumptions underlying workplace organisation and patterns of interaction . . . and learn to change underlying values. Through confronting the basic assumptions behind prevailing organisational norms, values, myths, hierarchies, and expectations, workers help prevent stagnation and dysfunctional habits.' (Brookfield, 1987:157)

He outlines a number of strategies for facilitating critical thinking, but warns that facilitators need to discuss the consequences (sometimes risks) of critical action with participants. Workers may be suspicious of employers' intentions. He cites Marsick's advice:

> 'She warns against blithely assuming that management edicts announcing the need for participatory workplaces will induce a corresponding change in workers' behaviours and attitudes, without those in positions of authority modelling the desired change.' (Brookfield, 1987:137–138)

Brookfield assumes that providers of education in the workplace are always aware themselves, of the implications of critical action. Providers need to understand the culture of the organisation they work within in order to asses the likely efficacy of a particular action, and workers who have confidence in their tutor may be able to share information in that regard. Often participants are adept at critical evaluation of their situation and more keenly aware than tutors, of the consequences of action.

Harvey Graff describes how naive instruction can result in students being set up to fail by encouraging action which can have no real effect. (Graff, 1979) James Turk warns that literacy programs can be a useful means toward personal and collective empowerment in confronting daily issues, but that they can only accomplish this when they are specifically designed to empower the participants. (Turk and Unda, 1991:268)

Literacy: individual or social problem?

Government policy documents and management texts reviewed here generally agree that literacy is an individual problem, and that improvement in literacy will enable people to find employment and better their economic circumstances. In not surprising contrast, critical theorists reject attempts to relate literacy to job prospects. This is part of what Graff calls the 'Literacy Myth.' (Graff, 1979) Critics conclude:

> 'that the 'problem' of illiteracy (can) not be separated from the larger structural problems of society in which it occurs.' (Street, 1984:.214)

He quotes Hunter and Harman:

> 'It is our conviction that a mere rearrangement of educational furniture is too simplistic an approach to the resolution of the social ad economic issues of which illiteracy is only a symptom.' (ibid:214)

Peter O'Connor warns:

> 'In the workplace, the good intentions of the critical theorist/researcher/ practitioner, if not monitored and constantly reviewed, can be as unwittingly oppressive or damaging as the more politically naive or conservative positions.' (O'Connor, 1994:263)

He explains:

> '. . in our enthusiasm we often raise to unrealistic levels workers' expectations in relation to what a literacy programme can offer. We offer job opportunities, promotion, and greater enjoyment of life, but tend not to warn of the limitations, or the possible abuses of such programmes . . .' (ibid)

It is important that providers assess the realistic possibilities for their student group, and develop curriculum accordingly. At the same time it is necessary to work to change negative attitudes of employers to open up promotional opportunities for workers.

Heeding the message of Aronowitz and Giroux, educational providers need to re-appropriate the concept of excellence, currently defined as basic skills, technical training, and classroom discipline, and redefine it. We need to ensure that more than lip service is paid to the 'management of diversity' in the workplace. If not, we are warned:

> *'When all access to the means of human survival have been captured by capitalist projects, human beings, of necessity, will seek training which moulds them into acceptable employees, perhaps at the expense of education which prepares them for democratic citizenship.'* (Humphries and Grice, 1995:227)

References

Social science

Aronowitz, S. and Giroux, H. (1985). *Education Under Siege: The Conservative, Liberal and Radical Debate over Schooling.* South Hadley, Massachusetts: Bergin and Garvey.

Brookfield, S. (1987). *Developing Critical Thinkers: Challenging Adults to Explore Alternative Ways of Thinking and Acting.* San Francisco: Jossey-Bass

Brown, M. (1994). Ed. *Literacies and the Workplace.* Geelong, Victoria: Deakin University.

Burgoyne, J. (1992). Creating a Learning Organisation. *RSA Journal.* Vol. CXL No. 5428 (April)

Burgoyne, J. (1993). The Competency Movement: Issues, Stakeholders and Prospects. *Personnel Review* 22 (6)

Burns, R. (1995). *The Adult Learner at Work.* Sydney: Business and Professional Publishing.

Collins, M. (1983) A Critical Analysis of Competency-Based Systems. In Adult Education. *Adult Education Quarterly.* 33 (3).

Collins, S. (1989). Workplace Literacy: *Corporate Tool or Worker Empowerment?* Social Policy, Vol 20 (1) Summer 1989. New York: City University

Cooper. (1992). Qualified for the Job: The New Vocationalism in Education. *Links,* 42 (Winter)

Falk, I. (1994). Collaborative Negotiation and Power: Vocational Education, Corporatism and Social Policy. In O'Connor, P. Ed. *Thinking Work* Sydney: ALBSAC.

Forrester, K., Payne, J. and Ward, K. (1995). *Workplace Learning.* Aldershot: Avebury Ashgate Publishing Ltd.

Freire, P. (1972). *Pedagogy of the Oppressed.* Harmondsworth: Penguin.

Freire, P. and Macedo, D. (1987). *Reading the Word and the World.* London: Routledge and Kegan Paul Ltd.

Gee, J. P. (1994a) *New Alignments and Old Literacies: From Fast Capitalism to the Canon.* Carlton: Australian Reading Association.

Gowen, S, G. (1992). *The Politics of Workplace Literacy.* New York: Teachers College Press.

Gowen, S, G. (1996). How the Reorganisation of Work Destroys Everyday Knowledge. In Hautecoeur, J.P. Ed. *Basic Education and Work: Alpha 96.* Toronto: UNESCO and Culture Concepts.

Graff, H. (1979). *The Literacy Myth: Literacy and Social Structure in the Nineteenth Century City.* New York: Academic Press.

Hirsch, F. (1977). *Social Limits to Growth.* London: Routledge and Kegan Paul.

Hull, G. (1992). *Their Chances? Slim and None: An Ethnographic Account of the Experiences of Low Income People of Color in a Vocational Education Programme and Work*. Berkeley: National Center for Research in Vocational Education.

Hull, G. (1994). Hearing Other Voices: A Critical Assessment of Popular Views on Literacy and Work. In O'Connor, P. Ed. *Thinking Work*. Sydney: ALBSAC.

Humphries, M. and Grice, S. (1995). Equal Employment Opportunity and the Management of Diversity. In Boxall, Ed. *The Challenge of Human Resource Management*. Auckland: Longman Paul.

Jackson, N. S. (1993a). Competence: A Game of Smoke and Mirrors: *Competencies: The Competencies Debate in Australian Education and Training*. Fyshwick ACT: The Australian College of Education.

Jackson, N, S. (1993b). If Competence is the Answer, What is the Question? *Australia and New Zealand Journal of Vocational Education Research*. 1 (1) Adelaide: National Council for Vocational and Educational Research.

Jarvis, V. and Prais, S. J. (1989). Two Nations of Shopkeepers: Training for Retailing in Britain and France. *National Institute Economic Review*. (May)

Lankshear, C. (1993). Functional Literacy from a Freirean Point of View. In McLaren, P. and Leonard, P. Eds. *Paulo Freire: A Critical Encounter*. London and New York: Routledge.

Lankshear, C. and Lawler, M. (1987). *Literacy, Schooling and Revolution* . London: Falmer Press.

Levine, K. (1982). Functional Literacy: Fond Illusions and False Economies. *Harvard Educational Review*, 52 (3)

Marsick, V.J. Ed. *Learning in the Workplace*. Beckenham, Kent: Croom Helm.

Mayo, M. and Thompson, J. (1995). *Adult Learning, Critical Intelligence and Social Change*. Leicester: NIACE.

O'Connor, P. (1994). *Thinking Work*. Sydney: ALBSAC.

Ooijens, J. (1994). *Literacy for Work Programs*. Amsterdam: John Benjamins Publishing Co.

Saunders, M. (1995a). The Integrative Principle: Higher Education and Work-Based Learning in the UK. *European Journal of Education*, 30 (2). Paris: European Institute of Education and Social Policy.

Saunders, M. (1995b) The Problem With Competence. Lancaster: unpublished manuscript, Lancaster University.

Street, B. (1984). *Literacy in Theory and Practice*. Cambridge: Cambridge University Press.

Toms, J. (1995). Competency-Based Training: Methodology or Ideology? A Critical Approach. *Critical Forum*, 4(2) Leichhardt: ALBSAC.

Turk, J. and Unda, J. (1991). So We Can Make Our Voices Heard: The Ontario Federation of Labor's BEST Project on Worker Literacy. In Taylor, M., Lewe, G. and Draper, J. Eds. *Basic Skills for the Workplace* Toronto: Culture Concepts.

Velde, C. and Svensson, L. (1996). *The Conception of Competence in Relation to Learning Processes and Change at Work*. Conference paper, Learning and Research in Working Life. Steyr, Austria.

Wright, S. (1994). 'It's a Job': Learning in a Public Service Office. *Issues in Work-Related Education*. Adelaide: Deakin University.

Management texts

Boxall, P. (1995). *The Challenge of Human Resource Management*. Auckland: Longman Paul.

Lloyd, C. and Cook, A. (1993). *Implementing Standards of Competence: Practical Strategies for Industry* . London: Kogan Page Ltd.

Peters, T. (1992). *Liberation Management: Necessary Disorganisation for the Nanosecond Nineties*. New York: Fawcett.

Senge, P. (1990). *The Fifth Discipline: The Art and Practice of the Learning Organisation*. New York: Doubleday.

Woodruffe, C. (1991). Competent By Any Other Name. *Personnel Management*. (Sept). London: Institute of Personnel Management.

Research/reports

Bailey, T. (1990). *Changes in the Nature and Structure of Work: Implications for Skill Requirements and Skills Formation* Berkeley: National Center for Research in Vocational Education.

Diehl, R. and Mikulecky, L. (1980). The Nature of Reading at Work. *Journal of Reading*, 24(3) Newark : International Reading Association.

McGivney, V. (1994). *Wasted Potential: Training and Career Progression for Part-Time and Temporary Workers*. Leicester: NIACE.

Phillipi, J. (1984). *Job-Specific Reading Skills: Reading Competencies Commonly Needed to Perform Tasks*. (Contract No. DAJ37–83-D-004). Army Continuing Education Services, US Army Europe.

Wickert, R. (1989). *No Single Measure: A Survey of Australian Adult Literacy* . Sydney: Institute of Technical and Adult Teacher Education, Sydney College of Advanced Education.

Policy documents

Carnevale, A. P., Gainer, L. J. and Meltzer, A. S. (1990). *Workplace Basics: The Skills Employers Want*. Washington DC: US Department of Labr, American Society for Training and Development.

Department of Education Employment and Training. (1991). *Australia's Language: The Australian Language and Literacy Policy. Companion Volume to the Policy Paper*. Canberra: Australian Government Publishing Service Australia

Drouin, M. J. (1990). *Workforce Literacy: An Economic Challenge for Canada*. Montreal: Hudson Institute.

Foyster, J. (1990). *Getting to Grips with Competency-Based Training and Assessment*. Leabrook: TAFE National Centre for Research and Development.

Jurmo, P. (1994). *Reinventing the NWLP*. Submission to the US Department of Education. East Brunswick: Learning Partnerships.

UNESCO. (1978). *Revised Recommendation Concerning the International Standardisation of Educational Statistics*. Paris: UNESCO.

Unions

Sarmiento, T. (1991). Do Workplace Literacy Programs Promote High Skills or Low Wages? Suggestion for Future Evaluations of Workplace Literacy Programs. *National Governors' Association Labor Notes*. 64 (7–11 July). Columbia: Centre for Policy Research, National Governors' Association.

Zacharias-Jutz, J. (1993). Workers' Education, Social Reconstruction, and Adult Education. *Adult Education Quarterly*, 43(2), 101–109.

Practice and guidelines

Field, L. (1990). *Skilling Australia* . Melbourne: Longman Cheshire.

Field, L. and Drysdale, D. (1991). *Training for Competence*. London: Kogan Page.

Imel, S. and Kerka, S. (1992) *Workplace Literacy: A Guide to the Literature and Resources.* Columbus, Ohio: ERIC Clearinghouse on Adult, Career and Vocational Education.

Jurmo, P. (1995). Curriculum: Creating Multiple Learning Opportunities. *Technical Notes* New York: New York State Education Department. Workplace Education Project.

Phillipi, J. (1988). Matching Literacy to Job Training: Some applications for Military Programs. *Journal of Reading,* 31(7) Newark: International Reading Association.

Prince, D. (1992). *Literacy in the Workplace*. Surrey Hills: Curriculum Support Unit, Adult Migrant Education Service.

Schultz, K. (1992). *Training for Basic Skills or Educating Workers? Changing Conceptions of Workplace Literacy Programs.* Berkeley: National Centre for Research in Vocational Education.

PART TWO
ANNOTATIONS

Social science theory

1. Aronowitz, S. and DiFazio, W. (1994). *The Jobless Future,* Minneapolis: University of Minnesota Press.

Discusses the passing of secure, long term employment and the move to 'disposable and throwaway workers.' Challenges the belief in training for a globally competitive workforce. Details the deskilling of jobs and the creation of a massive industrial reserve army situated in part time employment, and ' . . . the exclusion of vast portions of the underlying populations of all countries.' Concludes: 'Economic growth . . . is structurally unable . . . to overcome the job-reducing effects of technological and organisational changes.' Suggested solutions include a reduction in working hours/no reduction in pay, international co-ordination of labour demands and a guaranteed income (not welfare).

2. Aronowitz, S. and Giroux, H. (1985). *Education Under Siege: The Conservative, Liberal and Radical Debate over Schooling.* South Hadley, Massachusetts: Bergin and Garvey.

An important overview and critique of the conservative, liberal and radical debate over schooling. Discusses the crisis in education. Outlines the attack on education by the New Right, and the lack of argument from the left. The crisis is not inadequate literacy, but an inadequate public philosophy of education – enabling a take over by the right in which education comes to be understood as primarily instrumental to economic ends. Suggests new directions critics of the left might take in addressing this imbalance.

3. Bailey, T. (1990). *Changes in the Nature and Structure of Work: Implications for Skill Requirements and Skills Formation,* Berkeley: NCRVE, University of California.

Analysis of international industry trends based on case studies of four industrial sectors according to two dimensions: the shift from manufacturing to service-based economy, and whether oriented towards capital intensive mass production of standardised goods and services or labour intensive production of a more varied and customised product or service. Contrasts over-education thesis with life-cycle theories. Argues that current changes in markets, consumer demand, industrial structure, and the labour supply are having a particular effect on skills and work and that these changes are making it more difficult to use technology to reduce skills. The report suggests that despite the simplification of some tasks, work design changes in these industries have increased the intellectual and skill demands of the workforce. The report observes an 'accelerating interest by employers . . . in programs to strengthen basic literacy, numeracy, written and oral communication.' Suggests a greater integration of vocational and academic (involving problem solving and social skills) in schools and a greater coordination of college courses and work-based training.

4. Ball, S. (1990). *Politics and Policy Making in Education: Explorations in Policy Sociology,* London: Routledge.
Outlines three positions on education in UK: Old humanists/ liberals/conservatives, industrial trainers, and public educators; and claims that public educators are caught in between. Notes that since 1976 'a much more direct relationship between education and industry has been articulated . . .' and observes ' . . . the orientation of policy making towards the consumers of educa- tion – parents and industrialists' where education producers are excluded. Investigates the repositioning of education in relation to capital, in particular 'the role that education plays in the maintenance of the accumulation of capital.'

5. Braverman, H (1974). *Labour and Monopoly Capital: The Degradation of Work in the Twentieth Century.* London, New York: Monthly Review Press.
Examines the impact of technology and the organisation of capitalist production on workers in this century. Braverman is particularly interested the separation of conception and design from implementation of jobs (of managers from workers). He argues that management have adopted new technologies in order to deskill jobs and thereby gain greater control. This deskilling, he asserts, has amounted to the degradation of work for the majority of the working population. He includes what some writers have termed the 'new working class' in his analysis of alienating work, and views management's problems as problems of costs and controls: 'The solutions they will accept are only those which provide improve- ments in their labor costs and in their competitive positions domestically and in the world market.'

6. Brookfield, S. (1987). *Developing Critical Thinkers: Challenging Adults to explore alternative ways of thinking and acting.* San Francisco: Jossey-Bass.
Identifies effective strategies for facilitating critical thinking in adult learners. Includes a section on critical thinking in the workplace and underlines manage- ment and human resource concepts which support critical thinking. Suggests that critical thinking can be seen as the central element in improving organisational performance. Contrasts the development of critical thinking with behaviourist models. Notes almost exclusive bias towards managerial and executive learning with the 'Presumption . . . that critical reflection is the prerogative of managers, executives, and professionals.' Examines Workplace Democracy: from worker ownership to horizontal communication and the Quality of Working Life move- ment (QWL): workplace democracy without affecting ownership. Outlines a number of strategies for facilitating critical thinking, but warns that facilitators need to discuss the consequences (sometimes risks) of critical action with participants.

7. Brown, M. Ed.(1994). *Literacies and the Workplace: A Collection of Original Essays.* Geelong, Victoria: Deakin University, Australia.
Introduction by Mike Brown examines literacies in relation to the workplace, and advises that as educators we need to improve our 'literacies', our understanding of discourses in workplace reform and education. Discusses and critiques the competency agenda, noting its connection with scientific management (efficiency principles). Concerned about employers determining content and requirements and that it is sanctioned by trade union officials, stifling critical debate. Warns 'flexible learning' may become another way employers can intensify work.

Outlines a more democratic curriculum. Other contributors are Allan Levett and Colin Lankshear ('Literacies, Workplaces and the Demands of New Times')[17], Peter O'Connor ('Fears, Fantasies and Futures in Workers' Literacy'), Crina Virgona ('Language, Learning and the New Industry Context: Issues of Language and Power'), Rosie Wickert and Mike Baynham ('Just Like Farmland and Goldmines: Workplace Literacy in an Era of Long-Term Unemployment').

8. Burgoyne, J. (1992). *Creating a Learning Organisation.* (April).
Outlines and discusses three levels or 'degrees of learningfulness' in organisations. A Level One organisation remembers and reproduces its procedures (e.g. a bureaucracy). A Level Two organisation is an adaptive organisation which can 'change and adapt to meet the changing demands of markets,' and Level Three organisations can 'develop their context' in a way that assists 'the development and enrichment of the organisation's stakeholders, resources, trading partners.' This is the preferred model.

9 Burgoyne, J. (1993). *The Competency Movement: Issues, Stakeholders and Prospects.*
A critical examination of the competency movement and competency based training as currently promoted by government policy and implemented in workplaces. Suggests that the 'scientific' basis of the competency movement is behind and detached from the current received wisdom of the social sciences and that the explanation for this is probably political. He critiques levels of competence and warns that competency based training is in danger of being damaged or lost through over simplification.

10. Collins, S. (1989). *Workplace Literacy: Corporate Tool or Worker Empowerment? Social Policy,* 20, (1) Summer 1989.
Outlines how business has been able to dictate the terms of the educational debate and how education has moved from a 'nutritionist' and 'medicinal' view to one 'more explicitly oriented to the demands of capitalist rationality and the values of the market, often translated as the 'national interest.' 'Raises important questions about the purposes of this new educational movement, posing possible

right and left wing perspectives: Is it a chance to wrest control of socialisation and values and attitudes necessary to maintain labour peace? Or an opportunity to develop a more critical, creative, and militant workforce? Provides examples of industry indoctrination within education and quotes US government support of funding to industry for training. Collins agrees with the need to develop skills, but asks who should have that responsibility, and to what ends? She notes some good union-led programmes and recommends more, suggesting that unions could bargain for better wages and conditions if they were able to control the supply of educated labour. Recognises possibilities limited by 'more mobile and highly competitive international economy.' States the need for an international labour movement.

11. Darville, R. (1992). The Economic Push for Literacy: Expansive or Restrictive? in *Proceedings of Adult Literacy: An International Urban Perspective*, New York, UNESCO. Conference Paper.

From a 'popular' social justice perspective on literacy, examines the recent 'economic push for literacy. Analyses workplace literacy as the textual structuring of both production know-how and labour-management relations. Examines different workplace literacies under different management regimes – from traditional hierarchical management, severely restricting worker literacy, to newer management forms which devolve textual practices to workers in various ways. Warns of restrictions in competency-based pedagogy and in policy that supports only workplace or work-related programmes, excluding many learners. Recommends a participatory approach. Notes a danger in programmes being locked into immediate economic objectives.

12. Fingeret, A. (1988). *The Politics of Literacy: Choices for the Coming Decade.* Keynote address, Literacy Volunteers of America Conference, Albuquerque, New Mexico.

Voices the concern of literacy providers that economics is becoming the only legitimate rationale for literacy work: literacy for protecting the present rather than an investment in a better future. Discusses also the development of narrow, technical programs that train learners in the limited skills needed to increase profits but stop short of true literacy development.

13. Fingeret, A. and Jurmo, P. (1989). *Participatory Literacy Education: New Directions for Continuing Education.* New York: Jossey-Bass.

A topically focused sourcebook combining research findings on adult students and programmes with the practical experience of contributors. Reveals how participatory literacy education programmes can greatly enhance effectiveness. Uses case studies to demonstrate how this approach has been successfully implemented in a variety of settings including communities and workplaces. Shows how a transition might be made from a traditional approach to a more participatory one.

14. Forrester, K. (1993). *Developing a Learning Workforce*. Conference Proceedings. Leeds: Leeds University. UK.
Contributors include Keith Forrester, John Payne, Fiona Frank, Steve Wilkinson and Mary Hamilton. An examination of employee development programmes in Europe and North America. Outlines current debates and policy development, organisational change and the development of competence, the potential of quality circles, Ford EDAP, employers' views on the benefits and blocks to setting up workplace education and pedagogical issues.

15. Forrester, K., Payne, J. and Ward, K. (1995). *Workplace Learning*. Aldershot: Ashgate Publishing Ltd.
Issues raised include employers' responsibility for training and unrealistic targets. Compars problems of NVQs and short-term needs of employers with longer term needs of employees. Comments on low level of skills required through NVQs compared to Europe. Asserts competency-based model is an extreme form of reductionism. Urges union participation. Observes the contradictory processes of deskilling and reskilling and how blame is heaped on the failure of the education system to deliver a trained workforce. Outlines accelerated de-industrialisation since the 1970s and 1980s research interest in Japanese management practices and notes how the UK Manufacturing sector is seeking to increase the functional flexibility of work forces. Asserts training the peripheral workforce. Describes the fundamental antagonism between the desire for a curriculum informed by broad social and political issues and narrow vocational outcomes. Argues British workforce is less skilled, less flexible and less qualified than its international competitors. Notes a lack of social and political debate in the UK in recent years.

16. Foucault, M. (1981). The Order of Discourse. *Untying the text* London: Routledge and Kegan Paul.
Discusses discourse, which is the key concept in Foucault's theory of the relationship and inter-relationship between power and knowledge. Argues that knowledge and power are inseparable: 'Discourses are about . . . what can be said, and thought, but also about who can speak, when, where, and with what authority.' He examines the use of language by the New Right and shows how conflicting discourses may arise within a common language.

17. Freebody, P. and Welch, A. Eds. (1993). *Knowledge, Culture and Power.* Falmer Press. Pennsylvania: Falmer Press.
Poses and critiques four hypothetical arguments about literacy standards and claims economic restructuring is widening the gap between first and third world nations. Contributors are Freebody and Welch, Leslie Limage, Amir Hassanpour, Christine Walton, Nicholas Faraclas and Naihuwo Ahai, Krishna Kumar, Anna and John Kwan-Terry, James Collins, Colin Lankshear and Peter O'Connor. Examines the cultural and political dynamics underlying literacy, supplying case

studies focussing on its historical role and the maintenance and suppression of marginal groups. The concluding chapter discusses the literacy crises in Australia, North America and Europe. Examines policy documents, curriculum statements, school texts. and describes ideologies on which these textual materials draw, psychologizing of individual literacy and economic competence. Claims that Australian studies of literacy typically omit social class as an explanatory variable, ignore structural barriers. Claims arguments for a crisis deflect attention away from productive directions for reevaluation and reform, allow for domesticating the curriculum and that the discourse of literacy crisis is a confection. Wants to know whose crisis it really is, and who benefits from the solutions.

18.   Freire, P. and Macedo, D. (1987). *Reading the Word and the World.* London: Routledge and Kegan Paul Ltd.

Introduction by Henry Giroux, who supports Gramsci's notion that much literacy work produces and legitimates oppressive and exploitative social practices. Giroux criticises the appropriation of schooling for the needs and purposes of industry and the church. Suggests five necessary preconditions for critical literacy teaching, and warns of the danger of teachers becoming mere technicians. Freire and Macedo discuss what is meant by 'reading the world', coming to understand that education is not neutral, discovering in whose interests the word (and the world) is written, and 'rewriting' it. Outline how students might become literate about their own histories and environments, providing examples of lesson material.

Examines the myth of universality of education and the consequent blaming of the individual for failure. Notes various current approaches to literacy, and conclude by arguing for the concept of emancipatory literacy, which incorporates a radical pedagogy involving a critical understanding of 'overall goals for national reconstruction.'

19.   Gee, J. P. (1994a). *New Alignments and Old Literacies: From Fast Capitalism to the Canon.* Carlton South Victoria Australia: Australian Reading Association.

Explores the new management literature of 'fast capitalism', and observes how their intent is to transform and prescribe: 'They seek not to describe, but to create a reality.' [p.2] Focussing on the paradoxes that emerge such as that, despite the continuing search for greater perfection, perfection is finite. Again, commenting on the new emphasis on the 'knowledge worker', Gee details how fast capitalist texts are in the 'world making' business, where 'enchanted' workers are encouraged to buy into company goals. The paradox here is that workers rarely have the opportunity to influence these goals. He argues that 'the convergence of interests between educationally relevant cognitive science and our business texts is nearly complete and quite overt.' [p.9]

20.   Gee. J.P. (1994b). Quality, Science and the Lifeworld, *Critical Forum.* 3, (1). Leichhardt: ALBSAC.

Links the cognitive science Discourse with the Quality Discourse. Outlines joint positions: thinkers who can transfer their knowledge and skills to new situations and to problem solve and to use metacognitive strategies. Notes differences: The creation of trust and commitment and the problems with academic expertise. Claims both Discourses create a situation where learners/workers must buy in to a predetermined goal, or be outside of the system. Sets out the role of Critical Literacy in working towards Social Justice: Need to give 'post-capitalist subjects' a metalanguage to debate goals and understand the Discourses.

21.   Gee, J., Lankshear, C. and Hull, G. (1996). *The New Work Order.* St. Leonards: Allen and Unwin.

Gee, Hull and Lankshear frame a concept of a New Work Order emerging within the new global capitalism. Discusses: the rhetoric of 'fast capitalism', the alignment of education and the new capitalism, visionary leadership, the paradox of control and flexibility. Presents a case study of the training and implementation of teams, analysing the meaning of worker empowerment and self directed teams. The overt hegemony in business strategy (loyalty, commitment, allegiance) is discussed. Argues for the need to go beyond simple immersion in communities of practice, to be able to reflect and critique them. Provides a 'discourse map of society', particularly of schools and workplaces as communities of practice and potential sites of active learning.

22.   Gelpi, E. (1986). Creativity in Adult Education. *Adult Education, 59* (3)

Emphasises imagination and creativity rather than a narrow view of competence; and the need also for adult Education to be 'informed' rather than 'determined' by the workplace.

23.   Gowen, S. (1992). *The Politics of Workplace Literacy.* New York, Teachers College Press.

Sheryl Gowen's ethnographic study of a literacy programme for hospital workers is carried out over six months. She is an interviewer and observer during the designing phase of the programme, and a participant observer during implementation. Through these interviews and observations she describes in detail the political forces which influence programme management, design, worker attendance and success, and which determine how much workers can improve their prospects after attending literacy classes. Shows also how the varied communication and organisational skills of workers are respected in their communities and disregarded in the workplace. Concludes by calling for a more participatory model of workplace education, with all stakeholders, including the workers, posing problems and finding solutions.

24. Gowen, S. (1996). *How the Reorganisation of Work Destroys Everyday Knowledge.* Toronto: UNESCO

Discusses High Performance workplaces, TQM, and how Continuous Quality management has replaced Taylorism and Fordism as organising principles where workers have lost jobs or been relegated to temporary and contractual labour. Warns American labourers are being reduced to a workplace underclass. Discusses how shifts to 'Total Quality Management' and the implementation of 'Workplace Literacy' programmes have served to further marginalise and alienate two different communities of workers. Argues for the theoretical possibility that although TQ 'could mean changes to more democratic workplaces with shared governance', it empowers only to increase corporate profits. Closely examines a workplace 'moving towards total quality.' Critical of both organisational and provider responses to workplace literacy.

25. Graff, H. (1979). *The Literacy Myth: Literacy and Social Structure in the Nineteenth Century City.* New York: Academic Press

Challenges the belief that literacy produces certain social qualities and ends for individuals, such as self worth, social mobility, moral growth and personal achievement. Challenges perceptions that literacy can improve the community as a whole, engendering orderliness and a law abiding disposition, cultural enrichment and civilisation generally. Labels this view of literacy as 'the literacy myth'. Demonstrates, using specific case studies from nineteenth century writings, the extent of the myth. States social reality is much more complex than a simple, one-way cause and effect relationship suggests, and literacy alone is not responsible for good outcomes, nor illiteracy for the lack of them.

26. Graff, H. (1986). *The Legacies of Literacy: Continuities and Contradictions in Western Culture and Society.* Bloomington: Indiana University Press.

Suggests that the importance placed on literacy and the view that social and economic difficulties arise from the lack of it, is a myth: 'the literacy myth'. Points out that we need a consistent definition of literacy and consistent criteria for what skills it comprises. He comments that it is seen as 'A technology or set of techniques for communicating . . . decoding and reproducing written or printed materials'. Concludes: 'Literacy is neither the major problem, nor is it the main solution.'

27. Hautecoeur, J. Ed. (1996). *Basic Education and Work.* Toronto: UNESCO, Culture Concepts. Canada.

An exposé of critical issues in basic education and work. The aims of this edited book are to provide better documentation of different ways of thinking about work and education, to find better arguments for criticism of current education and training policy, and to reveal strategies for resisting capitalism's destruction of the planet's resources. Divided into six sections, it comprises: 1. a critique of literacy ideology and practice; 2. documentation of transition to learner-worker workshops; 3. comparison of four basic education experiences in terms of intervention; 4. an examination of education and training practised in a new type of socially useful enterprise; 6. an examination of the relationship between basic education and work in the post-modern context. The conclusion reports some suggestions and recommendations from a final seminar meeting of contributing authors, who include Sheryl Gowen, Jean Paul Hautecoeur, Jean-Marc Fontan and Eric Shragge.

28. Hull, G. (1994). Hearing Other Voices: A Critical Assessment of Popular Views of Literacy and Work. in O'Connor, P. Ed. *Thinking Work*. Leichhardt: ALBSAC.

Drawing from her own ethnographic research of a vocational programme in banking and finance, Hull examines and challenges characterisations of workplace (il)literacy, the deficit model, expanded definitions of basic skills, costs to industry and the country, the value of functional context training, and the persuasive logic of current popular views. She argues that the popular discourse of workplace literacy underestimates and undervalues human potential and mis-characterises literacy as a single curative. Further, the discourse obscures other social and economic problems. She poses an alternative picture of the real potential (limitations) of literacy instruction, and asks 'What must we be concerned with, besides literacy, if we want to improve the conditions and products of work?' and urges us to listen to other voices. This paper appears also in *Thinking Work*, O'Connor, P. Ed. (1994).

29. Jackson, N. S. (1991). Skills Training in Transition: Who Benefits? In *NOW in FE Newsletter*, April 1991. UK.

Claims Competency-Based Training is aimed at planned obsolescence for many workers and that the simple one-dimensional view of competence obscures the struggles of workers to retain their skills and power in the workplace. These issues are silenced, she says, because they have greater repercussions for society than pedagogic argument centred on the nature of competency and learning.

30. Jackson, N. (1993). If Competence is the Answer, What is the Question? *Australia and New Zealand Journal of Vocational Education Research, 1*(1).

Argues that the competency-based training and education (CBT/E) curriculum measures are primarily a tool of administrative rather than instructional reform in a political climate where efficiency, effectiveness and responsiveness have come to represent good management practice in educational institutions. Explains some effects, such as 'goal displacement', and critiques the argument that performance based objectives are worthwhile because they are observable, measurable and can be clearly specified in advance. Notes a shift in which instructors have now a support role as 'facilitators of objectives and implementors of instructional models determined by others' and a broader shift in the domain of needs, from learner to employer. Explains that CBE/T initiatives are led by a coalition of government and industry and that CBT appears to meet the needs of industry, be market-led and decentralised, and therefore conforms to the economic orthodoxy of our time. Jackson further claims CBT has not been shown to be effective in improving standards in industry but has been shown to be frustrating and costly. Concludes that the real aim is to make educators accountable and that CBT/E tells more about the adequacy of instruction and assessment than about the performance ability of individual students.

31. Lankshear, C. with Lawler, M. (1987). *Literacy, Schooling and Revolution.* London: Falmer Press.

Discusses the politics and examines concepts of literacy. Provides an account of historical developments, eg. of the working class struggle for 'proper' literacy in England in the eighteenth and nineteenth centuries. Shows how literacy as practised in schools historically and today is 'improper' in that it discourages critical analysis, subordinating workers and students. Critiques competency based education,with its goal of developing a level of occupational knowledge which will enable adults to secure employment in accordance with their individual needs and interests, i.e. to understand and to follow. Contrasts this view with Freire's model of critical literacy which 'positively assumes the operation of structured oppression.' Finally describes a better literacy policy and practice in the example of the Nicaraguan Literacy Campaign, with sample lessons from texts used.

32. Lankshear, C. (1993). Functional Literacy from a Freirean Point of View. In McLaren, P. and Leonard, P. Eds. *Paulo Freire: A Critical Encounter.* London and New York: Routledge.

Describes functional literacy as essentially minimal, negative (avoiding failure), and passive (responding to outside demands), where people are helped merely to cope with their world. Claims this is 'banking' education, with learners as specta-tors. Argues functionally illiterate adults treated as the pathology of the healthy society. Examines APL (Adult Performance Level) Study programme developed by the University of Texas (1975) and finds it to be (unwittingly) guilty of banking education, false generosity etc. Suggests a humanising model of Functional Literacy and advocates the use of Freirean techniques across various literacy settings.

33. Lave, J. and Wenger, E. (1991). *Situated Learning: Legitimate peripheral participation.* Cambridge:Cambridge University Press.

Places emphasis on the whole person and the social character of learning. Challenges the assumption that learning is the reception of factual knowledge or information. Asserts learning is a process of participation in communities of practice – the relationship between learning and the social situations in which it occurs. Defines learning as relative to actional contexts, mediated by the differ-ences of perspective among co-participants. Describes a number of forms of apprenticeship. Concludes by asking what opportunities, in specific settings, exist for knowing in practice and referring to problems of power, access, and transparency.

34. Levett, A. and Lankshear, C. (1994). Literacies, Workplaces and the Demands of New Times. in Brown, M. Ed. *Literacies and the Workplace: A collection of Original Essays.* Deakin University Press. Adelaide. Australia.
Asks whether Australia's approach to literacy is focussed on functional, human capital requirements of industry or on a wider, more socially just recognition that humans have a right to lifelong learning, and concludes it is the latter. Notes that the 'New Times' have 'upped the ante ' for literacy, but that the required level of knowledge and skills has been raised for all basic education. Sees a developing fourth stage in modern formal education. Distinguishes between performance literacy and conscious knowing i.e. of why one is performing it, and how it relates to other tasks that are part of the larger process. Quotes McCormack: 'adults with literacy problems do not need something called literacy. They need education.'

35. Levine, K. (1982). Functional Literacy: Fond Illusions and False Economies. *Harvard Educational Review, 52* (3).
Criticises UNESCO and other assertions that relatively low levels of literacy will result in universally desired outcomes such as employment and economic growth, job advancement and social integration, maintaining that functional literacy rarely produces these goals. Questions the assumption that literacy is desirable for everyone even in societies where print materials are not widely in use. Attempts to trace the origin of the concept of 'functional literacy.'

Concludes 'It is difficult . . . to reconstruct the process by which functional literacy became synonymous with literacy for work . . . the new thinking required a label that suggested the economic benefits that could be expected from investment in literacy.'

36. Levine, K. (1986). *The Social Context of Literacy.* London:Routledge Kegan Paul.
Outlines differences between competence studies of literacy, contextual, and critical-cultural studies and develops a critical-cultural approach. Identifies five major component dimensions: linguistic, technological, individual, distributional, and socio-cultural. Offers an historical perspective, including an account of the development of the term 'functional literacy' and records popular definitions. Describes the Nottinghamshire Literacy Scheme, commenting on job prospects, recruitment requirements, and selectors' negative stereotypes which equated, or strongly linked, low literacy with low intelligence. Describes political philosophies related to literacy i.e. as a right (left) and as a duty (conservative) and a shift to literacy as an economic value. Relates literacy to workplace skills

development. Lays out a table of five possible response types to literacy, depending on how literacy needs are seen.

37. Limage, L. (1993). Literacy Strategies: A View from the International Literacy Year Secretariat of UNESCO. in Freebody and Welch, Eds. *Knowledge Culture and Power: International Perspectives on Literacy as Policy and Practice.* London: Falmer Press.

Discusses the impact of International Literacy Year, noting that key players are moving away from simple slogans such as 'to eradicate illiteracy by 2000'. Notes the trend towards literacy becoming the responsibility of public sector with an alliance of private, voluntary agencies. Comments on inadequacy of standardised tests, grade levels as arbitrary assessments. Claims net result disappointing, learner motivation neglected, because perceived as method of creating a more efficient workforce without concern for the needs and goals of individuals. Asserts successful programmes are based on three crucial factors: high level of national commitment, mobilisation of human and financial resources and popular participation.

38. McCormack, R. (1995). Different Angles: Thinking Through the Four Literacies. In Baker, P. et al, Eds. *Writing Our Practice* Melbourne: Adult, Community and Further Education Board.

Shows how the four literacies of the Victorian Accreditation Framework can be used as a tool for thinking and reflecting about Adult Literacy and Basic Education (ALBE). Offers different angles on the four literacies: personal identity, modern forms of knowledge, organisations and institutions (the workplace), citizenship. Claims the notion of 'Competence' is equal to 'literacy for practical purposes'. Describes 'modern bureaucratic organisations such as government services and workplaces, where the orientation is Literacy for Practical Purposes, but can offer personal development, political education, and bridging into further education and training.' Shows how all four literacies evade answerability. Comments on the view of modernity as separate domains (home, workplace, community, intellectual), post modernity as permeable domains. Analysis of literacy pedagogues: functional literacy, personal growth literacy, second chance education, critical literacy.

39. Mace, J. and Yarnit, M. Eds. (1987). *Time off to Learn: Paid educational leave and low paid workers.* London: Methuen.

Fifteen contributors. Includes contributions also from adult education students. Documents some of the initiatives which have enabled people in low paid jobs to access training. Points out that, by way of seminars, conferences and the like, salaried employees receive paid education leave (it is part of the job), but such privileges are denied to hourly paid workers, who must train in their own time. Concludes that Paid Educational Leave (PEL) is an important strategy for getting adult education to more of the people for whom it is intended.

40. Mace, J. and Wolfe, M. (1988). Women, Work and Release. *Adult Education, 61*(1)

Discusses PEL (paid educational leave) for working class women. Notes how 'family responsibilities' means women putting others' needs before their own, and how families often oppose a woman's educational development. Observes that PEL is part of providing for equal opportunities, but points out the fear these women may have that such courses 'will reinforce stereotypes of low paid workers being stupid, and helpless, and thus being responsible for their own low status.' Mace warns of the importance of knowing the reasons, and in whose interests, we undertake workplace education.

41. Mace, J. (1992). *Talking about Literacy. Principles and practice of adult literacy education.* London: Routledge.

Argues that literacy for employment, in reality, comprises many kinds of literacy, depending on the job, the organisation and the economic context of the work; and what an employer thinks they may need their employees to be able to read and write at work may not be what those people think they want to be able to do.

Asserts that the full range of literacy purposes and possibilities available to any of us has barely been described, let alone promoted. Adds that while the benefits of literacy remain vague, the disadvantages and difficulty of investing time in acquiring it are sometimes overpowering. Distinguishes between 'indispensable' and 'desirable' literacy.

42. Mayo, M. and Thompson, J. Eds. (1995). *Adult Learning, Critical Intelligence and Social Change.* Leicester: NIACE.

This edited book, with twenty-four contributors, offers critical approaches to adult education issues in the UK of the 1980s and 1990s, from a number of different perspectives. Discusses restructuring around market forces, 'moving away from education for transformation towards a narrower agenda of meeting vocational needs.' Focusses on issues such as competencies, equal opportunities, women's education, community education, vocational education, trade union education, the 'quality' initiative and adult learning in the context of global, neo-liberal economic policies.

43. NIACE. (1994). Workplace Learning. *Adults Learning, 5*(May), Leicester: NIACE.

A collection of articles, with a foreword by Charles Handy, published as a contribution to Adult Learners' Week, 1994. Reflecting the different experiences of educators and employers, the journal looks at vocational training and employee development schemes, lifelong learning, national targets and broader approaches to workplace learning. Contributors include Fiona Frank, Jill Mannion-Brunt and Pam Gibson.

44. O'Connor, P. (1993). Workplace Literacy in Australia. In Freebody, P. and Welch, A. Eds. *Knowledge, Culture and Power: International Perspectives on Literacy as Policy and Practice*. Bristol: Falmer Press.

Explores the 'economically competitive' argument and the effect of international Literacy year in accelerating the process. Asserts union ineffectiveness except to negotiate training development of workplace basic skills in Australia. Critiques functionalist approach, definitions. Also notes the common failure to see literacy as integral to gender and culture, the attitude to women and other marginalised workers, the 'veneer of tripartism', user pays, access. Urges more work needs to be done by governments to develop 'clear and just policies' on extent, conditions, standards and resource levels of basic skills education. States a need for education activists to clarify their perspectives of workplace basic skills education and to play larger role in the debate. Outlines good workplace basic skills practice.

45. O'Connor, P. (1994) Ed. *Thinking Work*. 1. Leichhardt: ALBSAC

This volume of writings brings together leading international theorists in critical literacy, including James Paul Gee, Glynda Hull, Sheryl Gowen, Colin Lankshear, Peter O'Connor, Mary Kalantzis, Bill Cope, Ian Falk and others. In his introductory chapter, O'Connor warns of a 'dangerous conservatism' in workplace basic skills theory, policy and practice. He discusses 'fast capitalism' (post-capitalist new work organisation) and promoters of organisational change, the 'new freedoms' for workers: core-periphery jobs, flexibility, technology, enterprise bargaining – all a means of controlling the workforce, increasing income inequality.

Cautions about the 'cloak for discriminatory practices' of culture and diversity. Critiques competency-based training and individual skills acquisition, 'skills deficits' and of worker 'empowerment' through total quality management. Invites workplace basic skills educators to contribute to changing the current (narrow) picture of workplace education. These themes are expanded by other contributing authors.

Glynda Hull examines popular views of literacy and work and Sheryl Gowen shows how educational policies and workplace structures contribute to workers remaining in entry level jobs. Colin Lankshear looks at the shared language of education and fast capitalism, in particular 'empowerment' and 'self directed learning.' He argues for stakeholders in workplace basic skills education to be aware of the different ways in which such concepts are understood. Through a transcript of a classroom adult community education lesson, Ian Falk argues that 'negotiated' classroom practice can yet amount to 'jointly reconstructing an acceptance of the teacher's pre-selected activities.' In summing up, O'Connor urges educators working in the area of workplace literacy to 'learn to read the world that workers inhabit, and to contribute to the development of learning responses based on that reading.'

46. Ooijens, J. (1994). *Literacy for Work Programs*. Amsterdam: John Benjamins Publishing Co.
Outline of changing ideas on literacy since 1960s. Contrasts Freire's conscientisation approach and Maguerez' work-oriented alphabeticalisation approach. Experimental World Literacy Program (EWLP) aims critiqued. (1970s). Traces 'functional literacy' as it came to include political, economic, social and cultural dimensions. Recommends Participatory techniques . Concludes that 'the dichotomy between emphasis on social aspects and conscientisation on the one hand, and productive aspects on the other, should be abandoned.'

47. Pollert, A. (1987). *The Flexible Firm: A Model in Search of a Reality*. Warwick Papers in Industrial Relations. (19). Coventry: Warwick University
Examines the New Times workplace and finds it consists of a small core workforce and a larger peripheral workforce of part time and casual labour. This thesis examines the way 'flexibility' is used in these high performance organisations.

Details the way flexible practices actually erode the pay and conditions of workers, particularly women and ethnic 'minorities.' Cites management strategies such as lowering labour costs, rationalisation and a just-in-time approach to labour utilisation.

48. Prinsloo, M. and Breuer, M. Eds. (1996). *The Social Uses of Literacy: Theory and Practice in Contemporary South Africa*. Bertram, South Africa: Sached Books and Amsterdam: John Benjamins.
'This book explores the social uses of literacy in a variety of settings in South Africa. It provides a challenge to an assumption in education policy that those without schooling represent a homogeneous and disabled group. The chapters are situated in post-apartheid South Africa's attempt to develop mass provision for adult literacy education. Such demand was policy-led rather than consumer-led, and as the chapters of the book reveal, the failure to understand the embedded nature of literacy use by various communities limited their influence and effect. The chapters are grouped in three sections: Literacies at Work; Mediating Literacies; and Contextualising Literacies. Together they represent a major addition to the work on understanding the meanings literacy has for people in their lives.' (In Hall, N. Ed., 1997:23).

49. Saunders, M. (1995). *The Problem with Competence*. Unpublished paper, Centre for Education and Training, Education Research, Lancaster University
Argues for situated competence embodying a holistic understanding of social relationships and cultural practices. Competence, he maintains, is uneasily placed between training and qualifying, and claims: 'There is no sense in a system which simply leaves the working population with the skills they already have, even if they are now able to produce a certificate to show that this is the case.' Advocates a notion of capability, embodying more than observable skills.

50. Stein, S. G. (1991). *Workplace Literacy and the Transformation of the American Workplace: A Model for Effective Practice.*
Proposes an alternative interpretation from a narrow focus of workplace literacy. Questions whether workplace education represents an effective strategy for overcoming traditional barriers to participation and success. Urges integrated policy response. Advocates the teaching of skills as generalised, polyvalent resources that can be put to many different and future resources. Recommends participatory approach. Asks whether literacy audits could produce inhumane results, as debased as Taylorism and suggests they are not appropriate, with emphasis on task analysis and individual performance, to the new workplace. Outlines Massachusetts partnership in designing impact evaluation. Concludes: political leadership is necessary for creating a framework for addressing the challenges of the new economy that acknowledges the broad educational needs of the workforce.

51. Sticht, T. G. and Mikulecky, L. (1984). *Job-Related Basic Skills: Cases and Conclusions.* Ohio: National Centre for Research in Vocational Education
A pioneer of the functional context approach in the workplace, Sticht describes it as ' . . . instruction design using materials, books, tools and language of the working environment adjusted to the knowledge and experience of the student.' Claims this approach is more economical and more efficient than teaching decontextualised basic skills first then tying them to job skills. Discusses costs of establishing literacy programmes in the workplace, but is enthusiastic about outcomes. Maintains that where workers have used job-specific materials to improve reading skills, effects of instruction proved less susceptible to attrition over time.

52. Street, B. (1984). *Literacy in Theory and Practice.* Cambridge: Cambridge University Press.
Explains and compares an 'autonomous model' with an 'ideological model' of literacy. Education systems, say supporters of the former model, develop 'intellectual competence' that would otherwise go largely undeveloped. Street shows how the premise on which the supportive research results are based, is flawed. Investigates the development of commercial literacy skills by Iranian villagers explores literacy as a socialisation process rather than as a technical process. Examines the Unesco literacy campaigns and their concern with economic productivity and argues ' . . . if 'intellectual competence' includes . . . critical consciousness, then it might well be in conflict with productivity.' Warns that some forms of literacy programme actually impair criticalness and that what is being imparted is not a technical skill but an ideology.

Street suggests the need for a more general theory of literacy practice. He posits an ideological model of literacy which makes explicit the dominant establishment uses of and assumptions about literacy in this culture. He shows how the work of ALBSU (now the Basic Skills Agency) in the UK goes some way towards an ideological model in that it is concerned with context and literacy practice, but warns that merely to enable students to make demands about their own educational needs does not mean that they will be enabled to change fundamental disadvantage.

53. Thompson, P. and McHugh, D. (1990). *Work Organisations.* London: The Macmillan Press Ltd.
Note much organisation 'theory' tends to be a mixture of analysis and prescription, and much has been ahistorical. Analyses theories and practices together as part of specific historical, economic and political contexts. Looks at studies which have a specific competence in the sphere of work organisations, which retain the capacity to cross discipline boundaries, and which combine theoretical and practical emphasis. Attempts to identify the best known theories of organisations eg. Taylorism, and learning from Japan. Examines corporate cultures as possible attempts to constitute a form of 'organisation man.' Investigates how management and other groups shape and regulate identities and subjectivity of employees.

54. Toms, J. (1995). Competency-Based Training: Methodology or Ideology? A Critical Approach. *Critical Forum.* Vol.4, (2). Leichhardt: ALBSAC.
Notes the paradox in the definition of competencies as established by an alliance of business, bureaucrats and unions. Asserts that it draws heavily on behavioural psychology and is reductionist in that it reflects a systems approach, with one correct form of understanding, rather than an educational or social one. Comments on the affect of technology and flexibility in industry and the maintenance of gendered power relations. Real and perceived levels of skill downgraded. Describes competency based training as 'a tool to support capital accumulation.' and refers to its gate keeping function, imposing entry qualifications on jobs where previously none existed. Sees CBT as 'an attempt to qualify education as a production function analogous to the production of goods' and claims that it has the affect of ' . . . disenfranchising educators and stifling critical debate.'

55. Velde, C. and Svensson, L. (1996). *The Conception of Competence in Relation to Learning Processes and Change at Work.* The fourth Conference on Learning and Research in Working Life. Steyr, Austria.
Propose an alternative, holistic approach to competence. Argue that although competency-based training has some virtues from a policy point of view, guided as it is more by economic forces than educational ones, it can be condemned theoretically and methodologically. Note chief criticisms, eg. narrow in focus, that it defines knowledge in the light of bureaucratic and corporate needs, and deskilling of educator's role. Suggest a need to clarify the meaning of competence and to develop an alternative to the behaviouristic approach. Identify a 'relational model' which 'attempts to locate competence within contextually located sets of social relations and their culture of practice.'

56. Watkins. (1991). *Knowledge and Control in the Flexible Workplace.* Geelong Victoria: Deakin University Press.
Argues that the view that high tech industries will require large numbers of workers with high tech skills is flawed and unsupported by the research. Referring to research, asserts that it seems unlikely that high technology will have great impact on the basic nature of the occupational society at least up to the year 2000. Reports projections that high technology industries will provide only 3–8% of the new jobs in the future economy.

Management texts

57. Boxall, P., Rudman, R. and Taylor, R. T. (1986). *Personnel Practice: Managing Human Resources.* Auckland: Longman Paul.
A collection of papers analysing problems and opportunities in labour management in New Zealand. Examines international debates in HRM including workforce management, work design, employee development. Discussion topics include policy choices and practice in New Zealand organisations, the Employment Contracts Act, and Total Quality Management.

58. Boyett, J. H. and Conn, H,P. (1992). *Workplace 2000: The Revolution Reshaping American Business.* New York: Plume Penguin.
Predicts that by the year 2000, business will dismantle its rigid hierarchies and 'ceremonial trappings of power,' because it will increase the competitive edge of a company. Hierarchy will be replaced by shared goals, company loyalty. Claims that since motivation is crucial, 'leaders', not bosses, will 'redirect follower behaviour in concert with the common good.'

59. Burns, R. (1995). *The Adult Learner at Work.* Sydney: Business and Professional Publishing.
Written by a psychologist, this book focusses on some of the effects of technological, structural and economic change in the workplace. Claims trainers and educators need a greater knowledge of psychology and describes ways organisations can transform themselves into learning organisations. Questions the relevance of the current training agenda and advocates a change in the way organisations view their human resources. Concurs with other authors who claim that workplace training and education is vital to increasing Australia's international competitiveness. Strongly critical of the CBT 'revolution', he offers a new definition of training which employs an understanding of the psychology of the learning process. Finally he outlines some training strategies involving integration and mentoring, and some tips on how to develop a true learning organisation.

60. Callister, P. (1990). *Tomorrow's Skills*. Wellington: New Zealand Planning Council.

Foreword by Hugh Fletcher, CEO of Fletcher Challenge Ltd, claims this publication clearly shows the need to upgrade skills across the whole economy. Looks at the position of NZ in the new world economy. Factors examines include the movement of employment from the production to the service sector, the move to information intensive jobs and to jobs requiring higher levels of education. Analyses the skills needed for this new situation and asserts that the number of young people in formal training is significantly lower than in most OECD countries. They deduce that the current NZ workforce is ill-equipped for the challenges of the new economy. Quote Tom Peters in urging better participation in education. They conclude that the challenges for Tomorrow's Schools are to improve participation rates and to make what is taught more relevant to the new economy.

61. Collard, R. (1993). *Total Quality Success through People*. London, Institute of Personnel Management.

Provides some information about the development of the total quality movement in Japan and elsewhere and warns that the UK has significant barriers to total quality in terms of attitude. Sets out the basic principles and provides guidelines for acting on those principles.

62. Drucker, P. F. (1993). *Post-Capitalist Society*. New York: Harper.

Peter Drucker provides his analysis of the movement from capitalism to what he calls the 'Knowledge Society'. Knowledge, he says, is now our most important product, and the challenge is to improve the productivity of knowledge workers. He concludes that today's schools are failing to provide the nation with a workforce capable of performing jobs adequately (1989), because they lack the necessary knowledge. Prescribes what he sees as the right kind of team, how best to restructure organisations, eg. to 'outsource' work. Criticises the apparent existing power of universities and hospitals and re-interprets an individual's contribution and loyalty to an organisation (here he is talking about profit-making organisations) as social responsibility.

63. Eurich, N. (1985). *Corporate Classrooms: The Learning Business*. Princeton: Carnegie Foundation for the Advancement of Teaching.

Addressed to corporate business, this work refers to statements by major industrial figures in its argument for workplace training. States that because US taxes support workplace education, and because workers have rights as citizens, employers should view education in the workplace as part of a larger educational and social context. However, the 'worker' referred to here wears a white collar. Urges collaboration with other sectors and more openness and public accountability.

64.   Handy, C. (1988). *Inside Organisations*. London: BBC Books.

Acclaimed as a classic text, with a dictionary of key concepts: culture, motivation, leadership, power, role playing and group working. Discusses 'Learning Organisations', referring to the shamrock theory of labour organisation and management, which has a core and peripheral workforce. Enthuses about the competitive advantage of organisations which encourage learning, relish curiosity, questions and ideas, allow space for experiment and for reflection, forgive mistakes and promote self-confidence. Offers guidelines for managers needing to select, develop and reward people, to structure and design their work, and to resolve political conflicts.

65.   Johnson, W. B. and Packer, A. E. (1987). *Workforce 2000: Work and Workers in the 21st Century*. New York: Hudson Institute

Predicts the US is going to be in serious trouble in the global marketplace if it does not do something about the education of its workforce. Documents labour patterns and social trends over the last decades and discovers a growing shift from manufacturing to service industries and accelerating education demands in the workplace. Warns of a 'serious gap' between new skills requirements e.g. written, oral, math and problem solving abilities, and the poor skills of those entering the labour force. Charts the change in occupational structure and notes that even the least skilled jobs will require a command of reading, computing, and thinking that was once only required of professionals. Recommends employers should play a part in the training of their work forces, and maintains that education is no longer a social justice issue, but about international competitiveness.

66.   Johnson, P. R. (1994). Brains, Heart and Courage: Keys to Empowerment and Self Directed Leadership. *Journal of Managerial Psychology*, 9.(2:94).

This paper sets out the effects of worker disempowerment on employers and the barriers to empowerment. It provides a definition of empowerment (a belief in one's power) and self directed leadership (more discretion and autonomy). Describes the benefits to managers of worker empowerment and shows management how to provide opportunities for their workers which will return employees who are less risk aversive, more flexible, and more innovative and creative.

67.   Omega. (1989). *Literacy in the Workplace: The Executive Perspective*. Bryn Mawr: Omega Group

Interviews with 28 executives, presenting two views: narrow context specific and expanded (including work skills literacy and personal literacy). Those surveyed perceived lack of responsibility and commitment, awareness and response as barriers to take up by workers and employers. Recommendations: position literacy as everybody's problem, inform schools and students, educate business as to how they can contribute, highlight advantages to business and successes to employees, additional funding and standardised achievement tests in schools.

68.   Reich, R. (1992). *The Work of Nations.* New York: Vintage Books

Claims that there is no longer such a thing as a national economy, that we can no longer afford to cling to economic nationalism in these new times of global communications and global organisations. Describes the global sourcing of cheap labour as a benefit (to overseas labour) but a cost to those at home who have no jobs or unions bargaining power across national borders. Sees this as an opportunity. Promotes the idea of a global economy.

69.   Senge, P. (1990). *The Fifth Discipline: The Art and Practice of the Learning Organisation.* New York: Doubleday

Advice on how to become a learning organisation so that you can learn faster than your competitors . . . [and have] a sustainable advantage. Outlines five learning disciplines: Systems thinking (fifth discipline), Personal mastery, Mental models, Building shared vision and Team learning. Prescribes to business leaders and employees how to improve their own effectiveness at work and the effectiveness of the organisation. Stresses the importance of understanding the goals of the organisation and being loyal to them. Promotes a concept of leader as designer, parent, steward, teacher, increasing individual choice.

70.   Wiggenhorn, W. (1990). Motorola U: When Training Becomes Education. *Harvard Business Review,* (July-August). [71–83].

Discusses Motorola's need for communication and computational skills to 7th grade, going up to 9th, people willing to work against quality and output instead of the time clock, education as continuous and participative, 'illiteracy' of the workforce. Sees motivation as an issue, and shared responsibility. States that change must begin at the top, and permeate through, to arrive at a common language of quality (eg. six sigma). Discusses Motorola U programmes where workers had a right to training, and were sacked if they refused. Discusses elements of curriculum: – culture, – remedial reading and maths. Outlines perceived returns for individual training investment – marketable skills, self-esteem, self-confidence. Reports Motorola U aims to focus on the needs of the individual as well as the needs of the organisation.

71.   Young, C. (1992). Workplace Reform: So Much To Gain. *New Zealand Business.* Auckland: NZ Business Journal.

This article promotes the benefits of companies getting involved in teams, communication and consultation and staff training, with an emphasis on high skill/high wages. Describes three companies engaged in workplace reform and training their workers to take responsibility for the way the company is run. Highlights their successes in terms of improved industrial relations and productivity.

Research reports

72. Bartell, A., Lichtenberg, F. and Vaughan, R. (1989). *Technological Change, Trade, and the need for educated employees: Implications for Policy.* New York: National Center on Education and Employment. Columbia University. 'Asserts that new technologies create work environments that demand more learning. High tech industries are likely to be influenced by the level of education of the local labor force and the quality of local education institutions. Therefore, the emerging patterns of international trade will reinforce the growing need for better educated workers'. [Carmen, 1995]

73. ALBSU. (1995). *Basic Skills Training at Work: A Study of Effectiveness* . London: ALBSU.
Examines the contribution that workplace training can make to improving basic skills of individuals and how this impacts on their work. Also considers indirect benefits of training programmes eg. on self esteem. Uses 17 employer-based case studies from a range of industries. Notes the general high degree of effectiveness in virtually all case studies and looks at how some practical constraints might be alleviated. Stresses the importance of management awareness and perceptions, to programme success.

74. Carnevale, A. P., Gainer, L. J. and Meltzer, A. S. (1990). *Workplace Basics: The Skills Employers Want.* Washington DC: US Department of Labour, American Society for Training and Development.
Based on employer needs and views on basic skills, outlines US military literacy testing. Lists and details expanded view of basic skills. Blames lack of training for non-supervisory levels of the workforce on US industry competing less well globally. Emphasises 'learning to learn.' Quotes reports of deficiencies in non-supervisory and production levels and inn secretarial, managerial and supervisory positions. Advocates task analysis, 'the applied approach' and competencies.

75. Confederation of British Industry. (1989). *Towards a Skills Revolution* London: CBI
Published by the Confederation of British Industry, this is a report of the vocational Education and Training Task Force. It recommends training targets and action, commenting on motivation and transferable skills. Describes the concept of 'Investors in People' and details how employers' performance could be improved by becoming investors in the training of their workforce.

76. Cornell, T. (1988). *Characteristics of Effective Occupational Literacy Programs. Journal of Reading,* (April). Vol. 31. Part 7. Newark: International Reading Association.
Observes rise in literacy programmes in the workplace, quotes statistics showing jobs requiring little or no literacy skills will soon disappear. Notes incidence and

value of partnerships. Outlines four steps to ensuring cost benefits: attention to training needs analyses; design of programmes; programme evaluations and impact evaluations. Sees concentration on literacy skills outside of workplace context as problematic because of difficulty of: 1. retention. 2. employer approval. Sees action-oriented tasks as the key. Advocates teaching to specific competencies.

77. Diehl, R. and Mikulecky, L. (1980). The Nature of Reading at Work. *Journal of Reading*. 24, 3. Newark: International Reading Association
Reports on results of a survey (Diehl) of functional literacy performance at work, within an acceptance of functional literacy and competency testing as desirable. Argues for a more accurate picture of functional literacy demands by a considera-tion of 'extra linguistic cues' (context). Findings: 99% of subjects do some reading at work; average of 113 minutes' (almost 2 hours') reading time; more job mate-rial read than any other in a day. Concludes that job-related literacy is the most important type. Suggests that because almost 80% of reading tasks are not felt to be necessary to the job (could do them with other help) perhaps it is not 'literacy demands' that are increasing, but 'literacy availability'. Notes that 'some research-ers . . . suggest that some jobs are closed unnecessarily to people with little educa-tion or poor reading abilities, based on a false estimate of the 'demands' of the job.' Observes that functional (meaning work) tasks are different to school tasks, and concludes that schools should not be expected to teach them.

78. Education and Training Support Agency. (1993). *Taking the Step to Skill New Zealand*. Wellington: ETSA and NZQA.
A handbook guide for employers outlining the concept and why employers should become involved. It explains the role of industry training organisations, and how the qualifications framework works. Finally it describes to government funding initiatives employers can take advantage of to train their staff.

79. Frank, F. and Hamilton, M. (1993). *Not Just a Number: The Role of Basic Skills Programmes in the Changing Workplace*. Lancaster: Lancaster University.
Investigates current developments in workplace schemes for adult basic skills training in the UK, and explores the attitudes of employers and others towards these developments. Identifies the conditions under which successful models may be implemented. Includes overviews of worker education in the nineteenth and twentieth centuries, and outline workplace case studies, a survey of employer attitudes, a discussion of benefits and blocks to setting up basic skills training in the workplace, an outline of the issues, and recommendations. Concludes that basic skill in the workplace does not exist in a vacuum, that it is an interdisciplinary topic, related to management and union concerns.

80. Hull, G. (1992). *Their Chances? Slim and None: An Ethnographic Account of the Experiences of Low Income People of Color in a Vocational Education Programme and Work.* National Center for Research in Vocational Education, Berkeley, USA.

A report of a three-year ethnographic study of the experiences of low income people of colour in a community college Banking and Finance vocational programme and at work. Outlines two polar perspectives on basic skills: preparation for jobs or preparation for citizenship. Explores how people experience vocational education programmes, and the relationship between those programmes, and linked jobs, to literacy and the current crisis rhetoric.

Includes interviews with students and tutor. Found skills needs stressed on the programme didn't match those needed on the job. Concludes: 'The problem is much more complicated than a deficit in skills, and its solution much more difficult than devising a new skills building program or providing workplace literacy instruction.' [p.61] Suggests how vocational programmes might be reorganised with a critical focus as preparation for citizenship in a democracy.

81. Jacob, E. (1986) Literacy Tasks and Production Line Work, in Borman, K.M. and Reisman, J. Eds. *Becoming a Worker.* [176–200]. Norwood: Ablex

Examines data gained about literacy activities from interviews with workers in production level jobs in two workplace sites at a milk processing and distribution plant. Claims results show that literacy tasks involve not only performing a job, but a network of related activities. Therefore literacy tasks seen not as ends in themselves but as means of performing some other tasks (reading to do) and are highly contextualised (only have meaning in specific workplace settings). Found non – contextualised literacy tasks were reported to be the most difficult. Offers suggestions based on the implications of the two studies and concludes: ' . . . literacy tasks that are part of training programs might be more difficult than those needed to do the job because the managers want to create the paper record they think they need to minimize their potential liabilities.'

82. McGivney, V. (1994). *Wasted Potential: Training and Career Progression for Part-Time and Temporary Workers.* Leicester: NIACE

Focusses on part-time and temporary women workers. Notes a substantial and accelerating increase in casualised employment and that the majority of part-time and temporary jobs in Britain are held by women, who are disadvantaged in promotion, and therefore have little incentive to train. Thus, she claims, a two-tier system of career development occurs. Notes training is offered mainly to full-time workers and that women experience the greatest range of constraints on their participation in training (lack of affordable child care, lack of information, lack of part-time training courses). Recommends policy initiatives to boost training for part-time workers eg. funding, and points to ' . . . the contradiction between having a flexible (part-time) workforce but an inflexible (full-time) training policy.'

83. Mikulecky, L. and Lloyd, P. (1993). *The Impact of Workplace Literacy Programmes: A New Model for Evaluating the Impact of Workplace Literacy Programmes.* Philadelphia: University of Pennsylvania.
This impact assessment model is based on studies of two workplace literacy programmes. It describes how to conduct evaluations in the workplace and impact assessments after the conclusion of programmes to asses learner gains and improvements in productivity. Data has been produced about learner gains, workplace improvements, and literacy related changes in learners' families.

84. Moore, L. and Benseman, J. (1993) *Literacy at Work: An Exploratory Survey of Literacy and Basic Education Needs in the Workplace.* Auckland: ARLA Workbase
A self-report survey of 17 related companies in the timber and construction industry, taken to investigate increasing reading, writing and maths requirements in the workplace. From 300 interviews with managers, supervisors and workers, the study found that although there was a significant discrepancy between management and worker perceptions of difficulties (management reported high needs – workers self-reported relatively low needs), the reasons for this discrepancy were not clear. The report makes a number of recommendations for increased and improved training policy and strategies including better coordination of industry training bodies and provision, identification of related competencies and qualifications and further research.

85. Tuckett, A. (1991). *Towards a Learning Workforce.* Leicester: NIACE
Invites the government to assume responsibility for creating a culture of learning, to legislate to establish an adult entitlement to education and training, to ensure resourcing of priority groups. Reviews current barriers to participation and evidence of what is being done now to meet the needs of the bulk of adult learners in the workforce, and makes a number of recommendations to government (learning targets, 30 hour entitlements, TEC budget contributions, tax relief, learning passports, personal tax relief for learning), and to employers.

86. Wickert, R (1989). *No Single Measure: A Survey of Australian Adult Literacy.* Sydney: Institute of Technical and Adult Teacher Education. Sydney College of Advanced Education.
Presents findings about the literacy proficiencies of a sample of 1500 adults aged 18 and over across all Australian states. Literacy is defined as 'using printed and written information to function in society, to achieve one's goals, and to develop one's knowledge and potential.' Sees literacy as a set of skills that people have to varying degrees, and samples the performance of tasks in relation to personal factors of age, level of education and English-speaking background. Samples are categorised according to one of three types of literacy proficiency: document literacy, prose literacy and quantitative literacy. The survey's findings supported other reports that occupational level correlates with literacy skills.

Policy documents

87. Benton, L. and Noyelle, T. (1992). *Adult Illiteracy and Economic Performance.* Centre for Educational Research and Innovation. Paris: Organisation for Economic Cooperation and Development. (OECD)
An examination of the experiences of different countries in developing workforce training. Linking economic performance to (il)literacy, the report focusses on a functional approach to workplace literacy and its assessment. Looks at the 'literacy gap' created by increased workplace demands.

88. Crowther, F. (1994). *The Workplace in Education.* Rydalmere: Edward Arnold
First yearbook of the Australian Council for Educational Administration (ACEA) Comments on changing work practices and their impact on Australian schools. Debates education and workplace practices. Asks questions about the nature of work in Australian society and about the impact of current changes in education and the affect of technology. Focusses mainly on schools, with two significant contributions related to Education, Training and Work.

89. DEET. (1991). *Australia's Language: The Australian Language and Literacy Policy.* Canberra: Australian Government Publishing Service
For implementation from 1992, this policy paper aims to 'enrich the intellectual and cultural vitality of [Australia], and to help secure our future economic well being'. Outlines goals and stresses the need for co-operation of state and territory governments, employers, unions and teaching professionals. Presents case for action, aiming to increase funding for general adult literacy provision, develop national literacy proficiency scales for the assessment of competency levels, establish consistent curriculum development and teacher training, and to promote Plain English documentation. Relevant factors quoted include workplace reform and award restructuring, competency-based training, the pace of technological change, lifelong learning, international economic competition. Links inadequate literacy to economic costs to industry, and to social costs. Explains benefits of award restructuring to employers and workers. Outlines the role of the states and territorial governments in training and education as well as that of the private sector, business and industry in the community. Stresses the need for businesses, as users, to be involved in policy development, certification and funding, and to develop a training ethos. Outlines Training Guarantee Act.

90. Department of Trade and Industry (1993). *Competitiveness. Helping Businesses to Win.* London: Government Policy document. HMSO. CM2563.
This white paper sets out the UK Government's proposals for improving economic competitiveness, and a 'snapshot of the work in hand'. Outlines the current position in relation to other countries in Europe and elsewhere, and looks at its role eg. in education and training, employment and finance for business.

Warns that the UK will be left behind if it does not develop innovative production, improve education and training, and reduce barriers for business. Promises support and encouragement for education and training initiatives and some financial incentives to business.

91. Drouin, M. J. (1990). *Workforce Literacy: An Economic Challenge for Canada* Montreal: Hudson Institute of Canada.
Provides a preliminary overview of literacy and workplace issues, examines related trends relevant to Canada, identifies linkages between workplace skills, economic trends, and workplace performance, and [Canada's] requirements by 2000. Offers an historical comparison: Taylor to human capital and screening theory and structural unemployment. Refers to the debate about the arbitrariness of equating functional literacy skills with a certain level of school attainment (e.g. grade 8–9), and the error of equating schooling with learning. States Canada lags behind in technological growth and there are likely to be increased pressures to accelerate. Argues a need to access continuous learning. States Canada will increasingly depend on events and decisions made elsewhere. Warns of the danger of a loss of best workers without training. Notes that the character of manufacturing industries is changing from production to service, requiring communications and cerebral skills. Observes a shift to longer learning hours, shorter working hours and a higher standard of living. Identifies three policy challenges: assessing and measuring functional literacy gaps, developing a continuous learning culture and identifying and understanding target groups. Concludes that human resources are the pivotal factor in economic growth for Canada.

92. Harman, D. and Lerche, R. (1988). *The Bottom Line: Basic Skills in the Workplace.* Washington, DC: Government Printing Office
Links basic skills to global competitiveness and urges the development of a flexible workforce: 'The bottom line for the public and private sectors is the best use of the nation's human resources.' Describes several successful programmes in terms of audits, partnership, design, outside provision, curriculum, motivation and personal goals, and describes four discrete areas for evaluation: 1. student reaction. 2. student learning. 3. student performance. 4. organisation results.

93. Jurmo, P. (1994). *Reinventing the NWLP.* Submission to the US Department of Education. East Brunswick: Learning Partnerships
Recommendations for the National Workplace Literacy Program, made to the US Department of Education in conjunction with the reauthorisation of the Adult Education Act. With twenty seven signatories, this paper was put together by workplace educators suggesting actions for strengthening and improving the National Workplace Literacy Program. Its requests include that assumptions on which the program is based be re-examined, and that a new workplace education model be developed. The paper lays out some of the problems with the current

model and outlines ways in which it might be improved. An excellent discussion document for providers.

94.   Keating, P. (1994). *Working Nation: The White Paper on Employment and Growth.* Canberra: Australian Government Publishing Service
The white paper outlines policy objectives for delivering 'employment and opportunity across urban, rural and regional Australia.' Emphasises the need for economic and social progress to go hand in hand. Lists financial commitments and explains the demands of global competition that require increased education and training. Underlines the importance of engaging industry in determining the direction of training reform.

95.   New Zealand Qualifications Authority. (1992). *Qualifications 21st Century.* Wellington: Victoria University, NZQA
Conference topics are: 'International Perspectives and Regional Issues', 'Assessment', 'Quality in Training and Education' and 'The Future Challenge.' Several speakers from the UK and Australia as well as New Zealand, drawn from educational institutions, industry and unions. Advise on developments in their own countries in terms of quality in education and industry, competency based training, and their views on the need for reform. Speakers from NZQA open and conclude the conference, explaining and promoting New Zealand's proposed Industry Skills Training Strategy as an example of how industry, education and government agency can work together so that, David Hood, CEO of NZQA, asserts: 'educational reform is an integral part of necessary organisational and economic restructuring.' [p508].

96.   UNESCO. (1976). *The Experimental World Literacy Programme: A Critical Assessment.* Paris: UNESCO
Examines the successes and implications of the EWLP, consisting of 11 pilot programmes around the world focussed on training in technological skills. Concludes that literacy programmes should be incorporated into and correlated with economic and social development plans, linked with economic priorities. For instance, they should aid in achieving main economic objectives, i.e. the increase in labour productivity and the diversification of the economy.

97.   Weiner, G. (1990). *Creating a Learning Culture: Work and Literacy in the Nineties.* Ottawa: National Literacy Secretariat
Summarises many of the findings of the report *Workplace Literacy: An Economic Challenge for Canada* by Druoin (1990). Outlines changes that affect Canadians as workers. Promotes the concept of lifelong learning as a means of dealing with the 'literacy challenge,' which includes the need to develop literacy skills in the 'illiterate' and to upgrade others' skills to meet new work demands. Quotes low reading skills statistics as examples of threat to Canadian workers. Urges development of 'cerebral skills' such as decision making and creativity. Concludes urgent

investment in education will result in higher employment, higher skills, higher pay.

Unions

98. Cornfield, D. (1987). *Workers, Managers, and Technological Change: Emerging Patterns of Labor Relations.* Plenum Press: New York.
Examines how workers and managers attempt to control the implementation and outcomes of technological change. Covers the post-World War Two changes to the present. Provides case studies of 14 industries in a range of economic sectors. Concerned with workplace control, analyses the impact of the new technologies on employment and collective bargaining and finds considerable erosion of trade union negotiating power.

99. Hawke, G. (1995). *Employment and the Future of Work.* Wellington: Institute of Policy Studies, Victoria University.
Conference papers from the Harkness Employment conference proceedings in Wellington on 9 and 10 of May 1995 aimed at workplace reform. Eighteen contributors from industry, government bodies, tertiary institutions and unions discuss international perspectives on employment issues, technology and employment, skills, globalisation, treaty issues and government responsibilities.

100. Hensley, S. (1993). Union Roles in Workplace Literacy in *Catalyst.* 23. (3).
Outlines labour's historical role in workplace literacy. Identifies an 'unprecedented number of worker education and training programmes' in 1980s. Notes low allocation of training budgets for production and assembly workers. (1989: 14%). One in 4 companies offering 'remedial reading, writing, or arithmetic courses.' Explains why unions are obvious trainers, concerned about workers' security, advancement, and basic wage levels. Details successful programmes and concludes that unions must put aside adversarial relationships, claiming that it is mutually beneficial for management and labour to be working together ' . . . to build a new American workplace in which mutual trust, fairness, respect, dignity, accountability, and responsibility are unalienable.'

101. Nygaard, K. (1980). *The Computer in the Workplace: Lessons From the Norwegian Experience.* Wellington: Industrial Relations Centre, Victoria University.
An occasional paper containing the essence of the presentation by the main speaker at a series of seminars conducted by the New Zealand Computer Society and the Industrial Relations Centre at Victoria University. Discusses the Norwegian experience of computers in the workplace and warns of some of the

disadvantages to workers. Lists a number of lessons that can be drawn from that experience for New Zealand workplaces and union participation.

102. Parker, M. and Slaughter, J. (1994). *Working Smart: A Union Guide to Participation Programmes and Reengineering*
Notes the paradox contained in the TQM rhetoric of respect for workers and worker participation and the reality of job overload and insecurity. Discusses trend toward management by stress, focussing on 'lean production.' Stresses factors noted include deskilling, strict standardisation of the way jobs are done, contracting out and feedback (monitoring) systems.

Participation programmes are a further apparatus for increasing worker cooperation.

103. Rainbird, H. (1990). *Training Matters*. Warwick: Basil Blackwell Ltd.
Examines trade union perceptions of the training opportunities offered to workers to retrain and update their skills when new technology is introduced in the workplace. Provides an analysis of the ways trade unions can and should organise around training issues. Covering initial training, retraining, the effects of new technology, flexible working practices, labour market deregulation and wider policy issues, it includes recent empirical research on nine major trade unions. She concludes that, while the introduction of technology has generally resulted in the deskilling of jobs, many trade unions now believe that demands for training may help guard against deskilling.

104. Sarmiento, T. (1991). Do Workplace Literacy Programs Promote High Skills or Low Wages? Suggestion for Future Evaluations of Workplace Literacy Programs. *National Governors' Association Labor Notes*, 64 (7–11 July). Columbia: Centre for Policy Research, National Governors' Association.
Compares 'low wage' and 'high skill' organisations, and finds 'low wage' organisations more prevalent in the USA. Describes how 'High skill' organisations tend to employ a broader concept of literacy than 'low wage' ones, and to be more democratic about programme planning. Argues that policy makers should support literacy programmes in high performance ('high skill') organisations.

105. Sarmiento, T. and Schurman, S. (1992). *A Job Linked Literacy Program for SPC: Are We Talking About Worker Training, Work Reorganisation, or More Equitable Workplaces?* (April) Michigan: The Work In America Institute.
Urges that high performance workplaces invest in radically restructured skill development programmes that are participatory and job-linked. He takes the position that to be successful, job-linked training must be worker-centred, reflect an equal partnership between union and management, and be part of a comprehensive view of the future.

106. Trades Union Congress. (1989). *Skills 2000*. London: Congress House
Sets out the trade union support for skills development for working people.States:
'To achieve . . . [economic] growth, individuals must be allowed and encouraged
to develop their competence throughout their working lives, through both
education and training . . . The training they undertake must be industry-led and
relevant to employment.' Asserts that vocational education and training must be
developed on a broad base of education in order to achieve a 'just and successful
economy, and a fair and progressive society'.

107. Trades Union Congress. (1993). *Working in Partnership for Quality Training*. London: Congress House
Examples of how Trade Unions in partnership with their local TEC/ LEC were
able to develop important training initiatives, especially for women, ethnic
minorities. 'The aim is to make sure that such an expansion in training
opportunities benefits everyone in the local labour market.'

Current practice/guidelines

108. Baylis, P. and Thomas, G. (1994). *English in the Workplace: Competency Framework* Surrey Hills: NSW Australian Migrant Education Service (AMES).
Describes some of the generic communication competencies required by
employees in Australian workplaces to meet language and literacy demands of
current employment and training. The competencies are described for a range of
employment levels and situations. Provides practical examples of how to identify
the language demands of work practices, gives a practical format for conducting
language and literacy assessments, and provides many examples of the kinds of
language and literacy competencies expected across a number of workplaces and
tasks.

109. Brooks, B. (1990). *Working Towards 2000: The Changing Nature of Work*. Sydney: CCH Australia Ltd.
This book is intended for student discussion. Overviews recent changes in the
Australian workplace, including technology, employment law, unions, new work
patterns. Discussion questions and exercises complete each chapter. The final
chapter details worker participation schemes, comparing Australian and European
practice. Also comments on the role of trade unions and education and training
for the future.

110. Field, L. (1990). *Skilling Australia*. Melbourne: Longman Cheshire.
A handbook for trainers and Technical and Further Education (TAFE) teachers, it
aims to 'supplement what others were doing to reform Australian industry and
improve the status and skill profiles of our workers..' The author attributes the

current 'serious' shortage of skilled labour to the neglect of skill formation policies. Provides definitions of a range of workplace learning terminology, including
competencies, multiskilling, skills audits, etc. Although the author acknowledges
the weaknesses of competency based training, he provides here a step-by-step
guide for for setting up such programmes.

111. Field, L. and Drysdale, D. (1991). *Training for Competence*. London:
Kogan Page.
Primarily a handbook for trainers, this book was first published in Australia under
the title *Skilling Australia*, for Technical and Further Education (TAFE) teachers.
The authors note that developments in Australia and other countries in training
have been similar and have adapted the earlier publication for the British market.
Covers main aspects of planning and conducting and assessing training in job
related skills. Incorporates approaches to skills training advocated by the British
government, the CBI and others which underpin the competence based
philosophy at the heart of the development of the NVQ framework. Discusses
'current skill shortages and links the process of skills formation to other aspects of
organisational technoculture', and terminology for describing jobs and skills.
Examines nature of workers skills, analyses changes in industry and implication
for trainers and further education teachers.

112. Imel, S. (1995). Workplace Literacy: Its Role in High Performance
Organisations. *ERIC Digest*. Ohio: Office of Educational Research and
Improvement.
Links a collaborative approach to workplace literacy with high performance
workplaces, seeing literacy as a potential agent for organisational change in high
performance workplaces, for the benefit of workers and management. Argues that
High Performance Work Organisations (HPWOs)' . . . need workers who can
take initiative, identify and solve problems, make decisions and identify and
engage in a wide range of tasks.' An expanded concept of literacy (including
teamwork), and the participatory planning process, it is argued, produces these
'high performance' workers. Outlines principles of good practice: involving all
stakeholders, empowerment model, respect for diversity, addressing other
workplace practices, tailoring curriculum to particular workplaces, Plain English,
voluntary participation. Concludes that although research supports the use of a
collaborative approach with HPWOs, it is not a sufficient condition, and workers
in HPWOs may still be disadvantaged.

113. Joyce, H. (1992). Pedagogy in the Context of Industrial Change –
Dependency or Choice? *Critical Forum*. Vol.1 (2). Leichhardt: ALBSAC
Discusses issues of dependency in the workplace. Urges tutors to: – 'examine
ideologies of education . . . perspectives and beliefs about literacy . . . assess the
role of language and literacy in a changing world . . . re-evaluate methodologies
in the classroom . . . understand the world which students need to access.'

Comments on Plain English approaches; restricted language means restricted workers. Advocates for the need to complete language analyses across workplaces to give prior knowledge and theoretical understandings . . . in order to be able to influence workplace agendas. Sees the teacher as central to the process of increasing the students' control over written language. Argues for the development of curricula which aim for access and inclusion into workplace literacy practices, by developing long-term goals of independence, rather than short-term goals that perpetuate the dependency of learners on other people to mediate for them.

114. Jurmo, P. (1994). *Workplace Education: Stakeholders' Expectations, Practitioners' Responses, and the Role Evaluation Might Play.* East Brunswick: Learning Partnerships

Focusses on evaluating workplace education programmes using a collaborative approach. Outlines the functional context methodology, but claims it is too limiting for emerging high performance organisations. Discusses the Quality of Work Life (QWL) movement which predates TQM, and which is the basis of this argument for more participatory basic education programmes. Presents a view of 'high performance workplaces' that is less sceptical than that of critical theorists who see them as potentially exploitative, and closer to the vision held by the QWL movement. Discusses what evaluation currently looks like, and sets out three evaluation models. Describes developments in the field and suggests ways in which employers, unions and workers can support these developments and improve their own understanding of the process.

115. Mawer, G. (1992). Developing New Competencies for Workplace Education. *Critical Forum,* 1(2). Leichhardt: ALBSAC

Examines the implications of industry restructuring for adult migrant English language programmes in the workplace in the context of competency based education and training. Discusses some changed demands on oral and written language as a result of restructuring. Explores the role of providers in the new environment and the issues they face.

116. Phillipi, J. (1988). Matching Literacy to Job Training: Some applications for Military Programs. *Journal of Reading,* 31(7). Newark: International Reading Association

Warns of a 'shrinking pool of qualified applicants for entry level jobs,' mainly minorities (Hispanics, Blacks, women) who have not gained 'employable' level of literacy. Reports estimates that by 2000, there will be more jobs than qualified people. Advocates training to avoid a two-tiered society, to qualify unemployed 'intermediate literates' for the job market. Quotes three job-specific literacy programmes carried out in the military, the common features of which are the goal of improved job performance and promotion, delivery based on prior task analysis, and the use of actual job reading materials. Suggests all these can be adapted to civilian programmes. Outlines how to teach job literacy, including in that programmes for employed and unemployed workers.

Emphasises the importance of teaching transferable literacy skills. Asserts that 'the cognitive process used to employ each competency is applicable to job literacy in 95 different occupations.' Finally, includes a suggested lesson format.

117. Schultz, K. (1992). *Training for Basic Skills or Educating Workers? Changing Conceptions of Workplace Literacy Programs*. Berkeley: National Centre for Research in Vocational Education.
Based on written descriptions of two model workplace education programmes (in service and manufacturing) examines assumptions contained in the reports. Explores conceptions of functional literacy. Argues that to define literacy as 'functional literacy' constrains curriculum and instruction. Suggests that a broader definition (as social practices and critique) is more appropriate to the new workplace. Notes that literacy audits and standardised tests similarly limit programmes and possibilities in a way that is essentially Tayloristic (breaking down of work into smallest elements). Comments that reorganised companies are asking learners to become active learners in the workplace and passive learners in the classroom. Concludes by offering five sets of matrices to conceptualise workplace education programmes, intended to help clarify the decisions made by programmes directors, the assumptions of various partners, and the range of possibilities.

118. Sefton, R., Waterhouse, P. and Deakin, R. (1994). *Breathing Life into Training: A Model of Integrated Training*. Melbourne: National Automotive Industry Training Board
This report documents the development and conduct of a series of pilot programmes based on accredited training in the Vehicle Industry, designed to support employee access, encourage successful participation and provide opportunities for language and literacy learning. Includes six detailed case studies which illustrate the application of the model of integrated training.

119. Stein, S. (1993). *Continuous Learning for Continuous Improvement or Basic Skills, Worker Empowerment and High Performance Organisations: Why You Can't Have One Without the Other*. Conference paper: Bridging the Skills Gap: Quality Connections for the Workplace. Dallas: Texas Consortium for Worker Education.
Advocates high wage/ high skills strategy. i.e. addressing the low wage problem by increasing skills through workplace education. Points out how companies who attempted to develop high quality workplaces, failed when there was no education programme in place. Argues that continuous improvement and ongoing, innovative, participatory education of the workforce go hand in hand (rather than short-fix, classroom based programmes), and that education should be part of the (continuous improvement) action. Links continuous improvement and high

performance workplaces to worker empowerment yet acknowledges that restructuring can result in ' . . . a very small island of high skill/high wage workers surrounded by a sea of unemployed.' [p.8].

120. US Department of Education. (1992). *Workplace Education: Voices From the Field.* Highlands, Massachusetts.
Report and guidelines from a 1991 conference on workplace education, comprising representatives from 39 National Workplace Literacy Program (NWLP)-funded programmes. A collaborative, partnership approach is stressed throughout. The report documents discussions of the four themes of the conference: Establishing a Strong Partnership, Curriculum, Recruitment, and Assessment and Evaluation, and examines future policy directions based on these discussions. Strategies for each theme are outlined, with an acknowledgement of common obstacles. The concluding chapter discusses the five most critical issues of workplace literacy identified by participants at the conference. They are: building effective partnerships, assessment and evaluation, curriculum design, professional development and funding. The notes are helpful guidelines for intending providers of workplace education and useful revision of issues, strategies and problems for those already practising.

PART THREE
BIBLIOGRAPHY

Bibliography

Bold figures preceding entries refer to annotations in Part Two. Italicised numbers at the end of entries indicate pages in Part One where the texts are mentioned.

Agger, B. (1989). *Fast Capitalism: A Critical Theory of Significance*. Urbana: University of Illinois. *18*

1. Aronowitz, S. and DiFazio, W. (1994). *The Jobless Future*. Minneapolis: University of Minnesota Press. *28, 50–51, 54–55*

2. Aronowitz, S., and Giroux, H. (1985). *Education Under Siege: The Conservative, Liberal and Radical Debate over Schooling*. South Hadley, Massachusetts: Bergin and Garvey. *19, 22, 30, 37–39, 76, 83*

Atkinson, J. (1985). Flexibility: Planning for an Uncertain Future. *Manpower Policy and Practice: The IMS Review* Brighton: IMS. *61*

Atkinson, J. (1988). Recent Changes in the Internal Labour Market Structure in the UK. In Buitelaar, W. Ed. *Technology at Work: Labour Studies in England, Germany and the Netherlands* Aldershot: Averbury Ashgate Publishing Ltd. *58*

Atkinson, J. and Gregory, D. (1986). A Flexible Future: Britain's Dual Labour Force. In *Marxism Today*. (April).

Atkinson, J. and Spilsbury, M. (1993). *Basic Skills and Jobs*. London: ALBSU/BSA.

Australian Chamber of Manufacturers. (1991). *Australian Chamber of Manufacturers: Education and Training Policy* .

3. Bailey, T. (1990). *Changes in the Nature and Structure of Work: Implications for Skill Requirements and Skills Formation*. Berkeley: National Center for Research in Vocational Education. *56–57, 71*

4. Ball, S. (1990). *Politics and Policy Making in Education: Explorations in Policy Sociology*. London: Routledge.

72. Bartell, A., Lichtenberg, F. and Vaughan, R. (1989). *Technological Change, Trade, and the Need for Educated Employees: Implications for Policy*. New York: National Center on Education and Employment, Columbia University.

Barton, D. (1994) *Literacy: An Introduction to the Ecology of Written Language*. Oxford: Blackwell. *13*

Barton, D. and Hamilton, M. (1998) *Local Literacies: Reading and Writing in One Community*. London: Routledge. *41*

73. ALBSU (1995). *Basic Skills Training at Work: A Study of Effectiveness*. London: ALBSU.

Basic Skills Agency. (1995). *The Cost to Industry: Basic Skills and the UK Workforce*. London: BSA.

108. Baylis, P. and Thomas, G. (1994). *English in the Workplace: Competency Framework* Surrey Hills, NSW: Adult Migrant Education Service.

Bell, D. (1974). *The Coming of Post Industrial Society: A venture in Social Forecasting*. London: Heinemann. *6*

87. Benton, L. and Noyelle, T. (1992). *Adult Illiteracy and Economic Performance*. . Centre for Educational Research and Innovation. Paris: Organisation for Economic Cooperation and Development.

57. Boxall, P., Rudman, R. and Taylor, R. T. (1986). *Personnel Practice: Managing Human Resources*. Auckland: Longman Paul.

Boxall, P. (1995). *The Challenge of Human Resource Management*. Auckland: Longman Paul. *79*

58. Boyett, J. H. and Conn, H. P. (1992). *Workplace 2000: The Revolution Reshaping American Business*. New York: Plume Penguin.   *19, 21–22, 30, 37, 49*

5. Braverman, H. (1974). *Labour and Monopoly Capital: The Degradation of Work in the Twentieth Century*. London, New York: Monthly Review Press.   *11, 17, 18, 20, 51, 56*

6. Brookfield, S. (1987). *Developing Critical Thinkers: Challenging Adults to Explore Alternative Ways of Thinking and Acting*. San Francisco: Jossey-Bass.   *42, 52, 59, 78, 82*

109. Brooks, B. (1990). *Working Towards 2000: The Changing Nature of Work*. Sydney: CCH Australia Ltd.   *50–51, 53–55, 58*

Brown, K. and Hubrich, L. (1995). Framework in Progress. *Learn*, 5(July). Wellington: NZQA.   *54*

7. Brown, M. Ed. (1994). *Literacies and the Workplace*. Geelong,Victoria: Deakin University.   *22, 68*

Buitelaar, W. (1988). *Technology and Work: Labour Studies in England, Germany and The Netherlands*. Aldershot: Brookfield

8. Burgoyne, J. (1992). Creating a Learning Organisation. *RSA Journal*. Vol. CXL No. 5428 (April)   *65, 67*

9. Burgoyne, J. (1993). The Competence Movement: Issues, Stakeholders and Prospects. *Personnel Review* 22 (6)   *52, 70–71*

59. Burns, R. (1995). *The Adult Learner at Work*. Sydney: Business and Professional Publishing.   *55, 57, 68, 72*

Burton, L. (1992). *Developing Resourceful Humans: Adult Education Within the Economic Context*. London: Routledge.   *53*

Business Council of Australia. (1993). *Flexibility in Training: A Proposal for an Enterprise Stream of Training within the Australian Vocational Certificate Training System*. Melbourne: BCA.

Business Council for Effective Literacy. (1988). *Functional Illiteracy Hurts Business*. New York: BCEL

Business Council for Effective Literacy. (1993). The Connection Between Employee Basic Skills and Productivity. *Workforce and Workplace Literacy Series*, 8 (March). New York: BCEL

60. Callister, P. (1990). *Tomorrow's Skills*. Wellington: NZ Planning Council.

Carmen, P. (1995) *Annotated Bibliography of Workplace Literacy Materials*. Washington DC: Office of Vocational and Adult Education.

74. Carnevale, A. P., Gainer, L. J. and Meltzer, A. S. (1990). *Workplace Basics: The Skills Employers Want*. Washington DC: US Department of Labor, American Society for Training and Development.   *29, 32–33, 48, 58, 66, 72*

Carnoy, M., Castells, M., Cohen, S. and Cardoso, F.H. (1993). *The New Global Economy in the Information Age: Reflections on our Changing World*. University Park, PA: The Pennsylvania State University Press.   *8*

61. Collard, R. (1993). *Total Quality Success Through People*. London: Institute of Personnel Management.   *39, 47*

Collins, M. (1983). A Critical Analysis of Competency-Based Systems in Adult Education. *Adult Education Quarterly.* 33 (3).   *70*

10. Collins, S. (1989) Workplace Literacy: Corporate Tool or Worker Empowerment? *Social Policy*, 20 (1) Summer. New York: City University.   *22, 65*

75. Confederation of British Industry. (1989). *Towards a Skills Revolution*. London: CBI.

Cooper. (1992). Qualified for the Job: The New Vocationalism in Education. *Links*, 42 (Winter)   *69*

76. Cornell, T. (1988). Characteristics of Effective Occupational Literacy Programs. *Journal of Reading.* (April). 31. Part 7. Newark: International Reading Association.

Corney, M. (1993). Aiming at the Wrong Target. *Training Tomorrow,* (June 1993).

98. Cornfield, D. (1987). *Workers, Managers, and Technological Change.* New York: Plenum Press.   *28–29, 54–55*

88. Crowther, F. (1994). *The Workplace in Education.* Rydalmere, Australia: Edward Arnold .

11. Darville, R. (1992). The Economic Push for Literacy: Expansive or Restrictive? In *Proceedings of Adult Literacy: An International Urban Perspective.* New York: UNESCO, Conference Paper.   *18, 20, 39, 41, 56*

Delgado-Gaitan, C. (1990). *Literacy for empowerment.* London: Falmer Press.   *9*

Deming, W. E. (1986). *Out of the Crisis.* Cambridge, Mass: MIT Center for Advanced Engineering Study.   *21*

Department of Employment, Education, and Training (1991a) *Australia's language: The Australian Language and Literacy Policy – The Policy Paper.* Canberra: Australian Government Publishing Service.

89. Department of Education Employment and Training. (1991). *Australia's Language: The Australian Language and Literacy Policy. Companion Volume to the Policy Paper.* Canberra: Australian Government Publishing Service Australia.

77. Diehl, R. and Mikulecky, L. (1980). The Nature of Reading at Work. *Journal of Reading,* 24 (3) Newark: International Reading Association.   *74*

91. Drouin, M. J. (1990). *Workforce Literacy: An Economic Challenge for Canada.* Montreal: Hudson Institute.   *20, 29, 31, 35, 51, 71*

62. Drucker, P. F. (1993). *Post-Capitalist Society.* New York: Harper.   *6, 22, 29–30, 39, 42, 46*

78. Education, Training and Support Agency. (1993). *Taking the Step to Skill New Zealand.* Wellington: ETSA and New Zealand Qualifications Authority.

63. Eurich, N. (1985). *Corporate Classrooms. The Learning Business.* Princeton: Carnegie Foundation for the Advancement of Teaching.   *53*

Falk, I. (1994). Collaborative Negotiation and Power: Vocational Education, Corporatism and Social Policy. In O'Connor, P. Ed. *Thinking Work.* Sydney: ALBSAC.   *76, 82*

110. Field, L. (1990). *Skilling Australia.* Melbourne: Longman Cheshire.   *17–18, 66–67*

111. Field, L. and Drysdale, D. (1991). *Training for Competence.* London: Kogan Page.   *40, 80*

12. Fingeret, H. A. (1988). *The Politics of Literacy: Choices for the Coming Decade.* Keynote Address, Literacy Volunteers of America Conference. Albuquerque, New Mexico.   *34*

13. Fingeret, H. A., and Jurmo, P. (1989). *Participatory Literacy Education: New Directions for Continuing Education.* New York: Jossey-Bass   *41*

Fontan, J. M. and Shragge, E. (1996). The Chic Resto-Pop: The Reaffirmation of Citizenship Through Socially Useful Work. In Hautecoeur, *Basic Education and Work: Alpha 96* Toronto: UNESCO and Culture Concepts.   *57*

14. Forrester, K. (1993). *Developing a Learning Workforce.* Conference Proceedings. Leeds: Leeds University.

15. Forrester, K., Payne, J. and Ward, K. (1995). *Workplace Learning.* Aldershot: Avebury Ashgate Publishing Ltd.   *18, 34, 42, 50, 52, 58, 65, 68*

16. Foucault, M. (1981). The Order of Discourse. *Untying the Text.* London: Routledge Kegan Paul.

Foyster, J. (1990). *Getting to Grips with Competency Based Training and Assessment.* Leabrook: TAFE National Centre for Research and Development. *66*

Frank, F. (1996) *Like a Cork Shooting Out of a Bottle: Students' Learning Journeys After Workplace Basic Skills Training Courses. A Follow Up Study.* Lancaster: CSET, Lancaster University.

79. Frank, F. and Hamilton, M. (1993). *Not Just a Number: The Role of Basic Skills Programmes in the Changing Workplace* Lancaster: CSET, Lancaster University.

Frank, F. and Hamilton, M. (1993). Warm Hearts or Cool Business? Employers' attitudes to workplace basic skills programmes. In Forrester, K. Ed. *Developing a Learning Workforce.* Conference Proceedings. Leeds: Leeds University. *49*

17. Freebody, P. and Welch, A. Eds. (1993). *Knowledge, Culture and Power: International Perspectives on Literacy as Policy and Practice.* Bristol: Falmer Press.

Freebody, P. and Welch, A. (1993) Individualisation and Domestication in Current Literacy Debates in Australia. In Freebody, P. and Welch, A. Eds. (1993) *Knowledge, Culture and Power: International Perspectives on Literacy as Policy and Practice.* Bristol: Falmer Press. *36*

Freire, P. (1972). *Pedagogy of the Oppressed.* Harmondsworth: Penguin. *11, 73*

18. Freire, P. and Macedo, D. (1987). *Reading the Word and the World.* London: Routledge and Kegan Paul Ltd. *12, 75, 77–78, 82*

French, E. (1982). *The Promotion of Literacy in South Africa.* Pretoria: Human Sciences Research Council Institute for Research Into Language and the Arts.

Garvey, J. (1992). *Literacy and the Remaking of the Working Class.* New York: UNESCO.

Gee, J. P. (1990). *Social Linguistics and Literacies: Ideology in Discourses* London: Falmer Press.

19. Gee, J. P. (1994a). *New Alignments and Old Literacies: From Fast Capitalism to the Canon.* Carlton: Australian Reading Association. *37, 52*

20. Gee, J. P. (1994b). Quality, Science and the Lifeworld. *Critical Forum.* 3 (1). Leichhardt: ALBSAC. *49*

Gee, J.P. (1996). *Social Linguistics and Literacies: Ideology in Discourses.* London: Taylor and Francis. 2nd edition. *1*

Gee, J.P. (1997). *The New Literacy Studies: A Retrospective View.* 'Situated Literacies' Conference paper, Lancaster University. *13*

21. Gee, J.P., Hull, G. and Lankshear, C. (1996). *The New Work Order:* Sydney : Allen and Unwin. *2, 17–19, 21, 29, 47–48, 51*

22. Gelpi, E. (1986). Creativity in Adult Education. *Adult Education,* 59 (3)

Goldberg, M. and Harvey, J. (1983). A Nation at Risk: The Report of the National Commission on Excellence in Education. *Phi Delta Kappan.* 65. (1). (Sept.)

Gowen, S. G. (1990). *Eyes on a Different Prize: A Critical Ethnography of a Workplace Literacy Program.* Atlanta: unpublished manuscript, Georgia State University. *41–42*

23. Gowen, S. G. (1992). *The Politics of Workplace Literacy.* New York: Teachers College Press. *35–36, 72*

24. Gowen, S. G. (1996). How the Reorganisation of Work Destroys Everyday Knowledge. In Hautecoeur, J.P. Ed. *Basic Education and Work: Alpha 96.* Toronto: UNESCO and Culture Concepts *17, 37, 49, 60, 76, 79*

25. Graff, H. (1979). *The Literacy Myth: Literacy and Social Structure in the Nineteenth Century City.* New York: Academic Press. *83*

26. Graff, H. (1986). *The Legacies of Literacy: Continuities and Contradictions in Western Culture and Society.* Bloomington: Indiana University Press. *16*

Gramsci, A. (1957). *The Modern Prince and Other Writings*. New York: New World Paperbacks.

Gramsci, A. (1971). *Selections from the Prison Notebooks*. Edited and translated by Q. Hoare and G. Nowell Smith. London: Lawrence and Wishart.   *75*

Hall, N. Ed. (1997) *The National Literacy Trust Guide to Books on Literacy Published During 1996*. London: The National Literacy Trust.

Hamilton, M. (1996). Adult Literacy and Basic Education. In Fieldhouse, R. Ed. *A Modern History of Adult Education*. Leicester: NIACE.   *15–16, 20, 41, 49*

64. Handy, C. (1988). *Inside Organisations*. London: BBC Books.

92. Harman, D. and Lerche, R. (1988). *The Bottom Line: Basic Skills in the Workplace*. New York: US Department of Education, US Department of Labor.   *21, 31, 33, 50, 83*

Harrison, R. (1992). *Employee Development*. London: Institute of Personnel Management.

Hart, K. (1991). Understanding Literacy in the Canadian Business context in Taylor, M. Ed. *Basic Skills for the Workplace* Toronto: Culture Concepts.

27. Hautecoeur, J. P. (1996). *Basic Education and Work: Alpha 96*. Toronto: UNESCO and Culture Concepts.

99. Hawke, G. (1995). *Employment and the Future of Work*. Wellington: Institute of Policy Studies, Victoria University.

100. Hensley, S. (1993). Union Roles in Workplace Literacy. In *Catalyst*. 3 (23).   *19*

Hirsch, F. (1977). *Social Limits to Growth*. London: Routledge and Kegan Paul.   *72*

Hirst, P. (1974) *Knowledge and the Curriculum*. London: Routledge and Kegan Paul.   *5*

Hoachander, E., Kaufman, P. and Wilen, E. (1990). *Indicators of Education and the Economy*. New York: Columbia University.

Huey, J. (1994). The New Post-Heroic Leadership. *Fortune*.   *49*

Hughes, K. (1995). Really Useful Knowledge. In Mayo, M. and Thompson, J. Eds. *Adult Learning, Critical Intelligence and Social Change* Leicester: NIACE.   *16, 22, 40, 57*

Hull, G. (1991a). *Examining the Relations of Literacy to Vocational Education and Work: An Ethnography of a Vocational Program in Banking and Finance*. Berkeley: University of California.   *34*

Hull, G. (1991b). *Hearing Other Voices: A Critical Assessment of Popular Views of Literacy and Work*. Berkeley, California: National Centre for Research in Vocational Education.

80. Hull, G. (1992). *Their Chances? Slim and None: An Ethnographic Account of the Experiences of Low Income People of Color in a Vocational Education Programme and Work*. Berkeley: National Center for Research in Vocational Education.   *72*

28. Hull, G. (1994). Hearing Other Voices: A Critical Assessment of Popular Views on Literacy and Work. In O'Connor, P. Ed. *Thinking Work*. Sydney: ALBSAC.   *36*

Humphries, M. and Grice, S. (1995). Equal Employment Opportunity and the Management of Diversity. In Boxall, P. Ed. *The Challenge of Human Resource Management*. Auckland: Longman Paul.   *84*

Hunter, C. and Harman, D. (1979). *Adult Literacy in the United States: A Report to the Ford Foundation*. New York: McGraw Hill.   *21, 83*

112. Imel, S. (1995). Workplace Literacy: Its Role in High Performance Organisations. *ERIC Digest*. Ohio: Office of Educational Research and Improvement.

Imel, S. and Kerka, S. (1992) *Workplace Literacy: A Guide to the Literature and Resources*. Columbus, Ohio: ERIC Clearinghouse on Adult, Career and Vocational Education.   *76*

Jackson, N. S. (1989). The Case Against Competence: The Impoverishment of Working Knowledge. *Our Schools/Ourselves* (April).

Jackson, N. S. (1991a). *Skills Formation and Gender Relations: The Politics of Who Knows What.* Geelong: Deakin University Press.

29. Jackson, N. S. (1991b). Skills Training in Transition: Who Benefits. NOW in *FE Newsletter.* (April).

Jackson, N.S. (1993a). Competence: A Game of Smoke and Mirrors? *Competencies: The Competencies Debate in Australian Education and Training.* Fyshwick ACT: The Australian College of Education.   *50*

30. Jackson, N. S. (1993b). If Competence is the Answer, What is the Question? *Australia and New Zealand Journal of Vocational Education Research.* 1 (1). Adelaide: National Council for Vocational and Educational Research.

81. Jacob, E. (1986). Literacy Tasks and Production Line Work. In Borman, K.S., and Reisman, J .Eds. *Becoming a Worker.* Norwood: Ablex.

Jarvis, V. and Prais, S.J. (1989). Two Nations of Shopkeepers: Training for Retailing in Britain and France. *National Institute Economic Review.* (May).   *68*

65. Johnson, W. B. and Packer, A. E. (1987). *Workforce 2000: Work and Workers in the 21st Century.* New York: Hudson Institute.   *28*

66. Johnson, P. R. (1994). Brains, Heart and Courage: Keys to Empowerment and Self Directed Leadership. *Journal of Managerial Psychology.* 9 (2).

Johnston, J. (1986). *Educating Managers: Executive Effectiveness Through Learning* . San Francisco: Jossey-Bass.

Jones, H.A. and Charnley, A.H. (1978). *Adult Literacy – A Study of its Impact.* Leicester: NIACE.   *12*

113. Joyce, H. (1992). Pedagogy in the Context of Industrial Change- Dependency or Choice? *Critical Forum.* 1(2). Leichhardt: ALBSC.

Jurmo, P and Fingeret, H. A. Eds. (1989). *Participatory Literacy Education.* San Francisco: Jossey-Bass.

93. Jurmo, P. (1994a). *Reinventing the NWLP.* Submission to the US Department of Education. East Brunswick: Learning Partnerships.

114. Jurmo, P. (1994b). *Workplace Education: Stakeholders' Expectations, Practitioners' Responses, and the Role Evaluation Might Play.* East Brunswick: Literacy Partnerships.

Jurmo, P. (1995). Curriculum: Creating Multiple Learning Opportunities. *Technical Notes* New York: New York State Education Department Workplace Education Project.

Kearns, D. and Doyle, D. (1991). *Winning the Brain Race: A Bold Plan to Make our Schools Competitive.* San Francisco: ICS Press.   *7*

94. Keating, P. (1994). *Working Nation: The White Paper on Employment and Growth.* Canberra: Australian Government Publishing Service.

Kirsch, I. et al. *Adult Literacy in America: A First Look at the Results of the National Adult Literacy Survey.* Washington DDC: US Department of Education, Office of Education, Research and Improvement.   *1–2*

Kozol, J. (1985) *Illiterate America.* New York: Anchor and Doubleday.

Kumazawa, M. and Yamada, J. (1989). Jobs and Skills under the Lifelong Nenko Employment Practice. In Wood, S. Ed. *The Transformation of Work* London: Unwin Hyman.

31. Lankshear, C. and Lawler, M. (1987). *Literacy, Schooling and Revolution.* London: Falmer Press.   *15–16, 68, 73, 77*

32. Lankshear, C. (1993). Functional Literacy from a Freirean Point of View. In

McLaren, P. and Leonard, P. Eds. *Paulo Freire: A Critical Encounter.* London and New York: Routledge.

Lankshear, C. (1994). Self Direction and Empowerment: Critical Language Awareness and the 'New Work Order'. In O'Connor, P. Ed. *Thinking Work.* Sydney: ALBSAC.   *49*

Lankshear, C. (1997). *Language and the New Capitalism. The International Journal of Inclusive Education.* 1 (3). In Press.   *2*

33. Lave, J. and Wenger, E. (1991). *Situated Learning: Legitimate Peripheral Participation.* Cambridge: Cambridge University Press.

Levett. A. and Lankshear, C. (1990) *Going for Gold: Priorities for Schooling in the 1990s.* Wellington: Brasell Press.   *6*

34. Levett, A. and Lankshear, C. (1994). Literacies, Workplaces and the Demands of New Times. In Brown, M. Ed. *Literacies and the Workplace: A collection of Original Essays.* Geelong, Adelaide: Deakin University Press.   *56*

35. Levine, K. (1982). Functional Literacy: Fond Illusions and False Economies. *Harvard Educational Review,* 52 (3).   *12, 72–75*

36. Levine, K. (1986). *The Social Context of Literacy* . London: Routledge and Kegan Paul Ltd.

37. Limage, L. (1993). Literacy Strategies: A View from the International Literacy Year Secretariat of UNESCO. In Freebody, P., and Welch, A. Eds. *Knowledge Culture and Power: International Perspectives on Literacy as Policy and Practice.* Bristol: Falmer Press.

Lloyd, C. and Cook, A. (1993). *Implementing Standards of Competence: Practical Strategies for Industry.* London: Kogan Page Ltd.   *67*

Luke, A. (1992). Literacy and Work in 'New Times'. *Open Letter,* 3 (1).   *34*

38. McCormack, R. (1995). Different Angles: Thinking Through the Four Literacies. In Baker, P. et al. Eds. *Writing Our Practice.* Melbourne: Adult, Community and Further Education Board.

McCormack, R. (1995). *The World of Work.* Melbourne: NLLIA Publications.

McGivney, V. (1990). *Education's for other people: Access to Education for non-participant adults: A research report.* Leicester: NIACE.

82. McGivney, V. (1994). *Wasted Potential: Training and Career Progression for Part-Time and Temporary Workers.* Leicester: NIACE.   *50, 73*

Mace, J. (1987) Adult Literacy: Campaigns and Movements. In Mace, J. and Yarnit, M. Eds. *Time off to Learn: Paid Educational Leave and Low Paid Workers.* London: Methuen.   *22*

Mace, J. (1992a). Love, Literacy and Labour. *Research and Practice in Adult Literacy,* Vol 17 (Spring).

41. Mace, J. (1992b). *Talking about Literacy. Principles and Practice of Adult Literacy Education.* London: Routledge.

Mace, J. (1993). 'A Spirit of Cordiality' Learning at Work: Perspectives and Participants. In Machell, J and Frank, F. *Learning at Work: Collected Papers.* Lancaster: Centre for the Study of Education and Training, Lancaster University.   *38*

40. Mace, J. and Wolfe, M. (1988). Women, Work and Release. *Adult Education,* 61(1).   *58, 61*

39. Mace, J. and Yarnit, M. Eds. (1987b). *Time off to Learn: Paid Educational Leave and Low Paid Workers.* London: Methuen

Macedo, D. (1996) Literacies of Power: What Americans are Not Allowed to Know. *Journal of Negro Education.* Vol 65 (2)   *19, 82*

Machell, J. and Frank, F. (1993). *Learning at Work: Collected Papers.* Lancaster: Centre for the Study of Education and Training, Lancaster University.

Manpower Services Commission. (1984). *A New Training Initiative. Modernisation of Occupational Training. A Positive Statement.* Sheffield: MSC.

Marsick, V.J. Ed. *Learning in the Workplace.* Beckenham, Kent: Croom Helm.   *52*

Mathews, J. (1989). *Tools of Change. New Technology and the Democratisation of Work.* . Sydney: Pluto Press.

Mawer, G. (1991). *Language Audits and Industry Restructuring.* Sydney: National Centre for English Language Teaching and Research.

115. Mawer, G. (1992). Developing New Competencies for Workplace Education. *Critical Forum,* 1(2) Leichhardt: ALBSAC.

Maxson, J. and Hair, B. (1990). *Managing Diversity: A Key to Building a Quality Woirkforce.* Columbus: National Alliance of Community and Technical Colleges.   *4*

42. Mayo, M. and Thompson, J. Eds. (1995). *Adult Learning, Critical Intelligence and Social Change.* Leicester: NIACE.   *69*

Mikulecky, L. (1982). Job Literacy: the relationship between school preparation and workplace actuality. *Reading Research Quarterly.* 17.

Mikulecky, L. (1996). *A Review of Recent Workplace Literacy Programs and a Projection of Future Challenges.* Philadelphia: National Centre of Adult Literacy.

Mikulecky, L and Drew, R. (1990). Basic Skills in the Workplace. *Constructs of Reader Process.* Unpublished manuscript, USA.   *41*

83. Mikulecky, L. and Lloyd, P. (1993). *The Impact of Workplace Literacy Programmes: A New Model for Evaluating the Impact of Workplace Literacy Programmes.* Philadelphia: National Centre on Adult Literacy.

Millar, L. (1992). *Literacy: At the Service of Human Rights Above All!* New York: UNESCO.

Montigny, G. (1991). *Adult Literacy in Canada: Results of a National Study.* Ottawa: Statistics Canada.   *20*

84. Moore, L. and Benseman, J. (1993). *Literacy at Work: An Exploratory Survey of Literacy and Basic Education Needs in the Workplace.* Auckland: ARLA Workbase.   *33*

National Academy of Science Task Force. (1984). *High Schools and the Changing Workplace: The Employers' View.* Washington DC: National Academy Press.

National Commission on Excellence in Education (1983). *A Nation at Risk. The Imperative for Educational Reform.* Washington DC: US Department of Education.

95. New Zealand Qualifications Authority. (1993). *Qualifications 21st Century.* 'Quality' Conference Papers. Wellington: Victoria University and NZQA.

43. NIACE (1994). Workplace Learning. *Adults Learning,* 5 (May) Leicester: NIACE.

101. Nygaard, K. (1980). *The Computer in the Workplace: Lessons From the Norwegian Experience* . Wellington: Industrial Relations Centre, Victoria University.   *53,55*

O'Connor, P. (1991). Trade Unions and Workers Literacy. *Literacy Broadsheet,* (33) (June).

O'Connor, P. (1992a). Choosing Sides in Workers' Literacy. *Critical Forum,* 1(2). Leichhardt, NSW Australia: ALBSAC.

O'Connor, P. (1992b). *Making it Happen: Developing Effective Workplace Basic Skills Training Programs.* Leichhardt: ALBSAC.   *40*

O'Connor, P. (1993a). Crossing the Borders of Workers' Literacy. *Focus: Adult Literacy and Basic Skills Action Coalition,* 3. Leichhardt: ALBSAC.

44. O'Connor, P. (1993b). Workplace Literacy in Australia. In Freebody, P. and Welch,

A. Eds. *Knowledge, Culture and Power: International Perspectives on Literacy as Policy and Practice*. Bristol: Falmer Press.

45. O'Connor, P. Ed. (1994). *Thinking Work*. Volume 1. Sydney: ALBSAC. *17, 21, 32, 35, 50–51, 57, 65, 69, 83*

67. Omega. (1989). *Literacy in the Workplace: The Executive Perspective*. Bryn Mawr: Omega Group. *56*

46. Ooijens, J. (1994). *Literacy for Work Programs*. Amsterdam: John Benjamins Publishing Co. *20, 77*

Oxenham, J. (1980). *Literacy: Writing, Reading and Social Organisation*. London: Routledge and Kegan Paul. *20*

102. Parker, M. and Slaughter, J. (1994). Working Smart: A Union Guide to Participation Programmes and Reengineering/With Union Strategy Guide. *Labor Notes*. (Nov.) *47*

Payne, J. (1993a) Employee Development and Lifelong Learning. In Machell, J. and Frank, F., Eds. *Learning at Work: Collected Papers*, Lancaster: Lancaster University.

Payne, J. (1993b). Learning at Work. Final report of the Leeds Adult Learners at Work Project. Leeds: Department of Adult Continuing Education, University of Leeds.

Payne, J. (1993c). Too Little of a Good Thing? *Adults Learning*, 4(10). Leicester: NIACE

Payne, J., Forrester, K. and Ward, K. (1993). *Adult Learners at Work: Perspectives on Training and Education at Work*. Leeds: University of Leeds.

Peters, T. (1992). *Liberation Management: Necessary Disorganisation for the Nanosecond Nineties*. New York: Fawcett. *49*

Peters, T. (1994). *Crazy Times Call for Crazy Organisations*. New York: Vintage Books. *46*

Phillipi, J. (1984). *Job-Specific Reading Skills: Reading Competencies Commonly Needed to Perform Tasks*. (Contract No. DAJ37–83-D-004). Army Continuing Education Services, US Army, Europe.

116. Phillipi, J. (1988). Matching Literacy to Job Training: Some applications for Military Programs. *Journal of Reading*, 31(7). Newark: International Reading Association. *71*

Pierce, G. (1991). Thinking Critically in the Workplace. In Taylor, M., Draper, J. and Lewe, G. Eds. *Basic Skills in the Workplace*. Toronto: Culture Concepts.

47. Pollert, A. (1987). *The Flexible Firm: A Model in Search of a Reality*. Warwick Papers in Industrial Relations (19) Coventry: Warwick University. *50, 58*

Popkewitz, T. (1991). *A Political Sociology of Educational Reform: Power/Knowledge in Teaching, Teacher Education and Research*. New York: Teachers' College Press. *9*

Prince, D. (1992). *Literacy in the Workplace*. Surrey Hills: Curriculum Support Unit. Adult Migrant Education Service. *79*

48. Prinsloo, M. and Breuer, M. Eds. (1996). *The Social Uses of Literacy: Theory and Practice in Contemporary South Africa*. Bertram, South Africa: Sached Books and Amsterdam: John Benjamins.

Probert, B. and Wajcman, J. (1988) Technological Change and the Future of Work. In *Journal of Industrial Relations*. (September) Sydney: Industrial Relations Society of Australia. *54–55*

103. Rainbird, H. (1990). *Training Matters*. Warwick: Basil Blackwell Ltd. *46, 50–52, 55–56, 58–59*

68. Reich, R. (1992). *The Work of Nations*. New York: Vintage Books. *6, 27–28*

Rogers, B. (1984) The Trend of Reading Standards Reassessed. *Educational Research*. 26 (3.) *16*

Sandelands, E. (1994). Industrial Training and Quality Initiatives. *Journal of European Industrial Training*, 18 (7).

Sarmiento, A. R. and Kay, A. (1990). *Worker Centred Learning: A Union Guide to Workplace Literacy*. Washington DC: AFL-CIO Human Resources Development Institute.

104. Sarmiento, T. (1991). Do Workplace Literacy Programs Promote High Skills or Low Wages? Suggestion for Future Evaluations of Workplace Literacy Programs. *National Governors' Association Labor Notes*, 64 (7–11 July). Columbia: Centre for Policy Research, National Governors' Association.　*60, 72*

105. Sarmiento, T. and Schurman, S. (1992). *A Job Linked Literacy Program for SPC: Are We Talking About Worker Training, Work Reorganisation, or More Equitable Workplaces?* Michigan: The Work in America Institute.　*40*

Saunders, M. (1995a). The Integrative Principle: Higher Education and Work-Based Learning in the UK. *European Journal of Education*, 30 (2). Paris: European Institute of Education and Social Policy.

49. Saunders, M. (1995b). *The Problem with Competence*. Lancaster: Unpublished paper, Lancaster University.

SCANS. (1992). *Earning a Living: A Blueprint for high performance. A SCANS report for America 2000*. Washington DC.

117. Schultz, K. (1992). *Training for Basic Skills or Educating Workers? Changing Conceptions of Workplace Literacy Programs*. Berkeley: National Centre for Research in Vocational Education.　*52, 79–80*

Scribner, S. (1987). Literacy in the Workplace. *Information UpdateLiteracy Assistance Center*, 4 (1).

118. Sefton, R., Waterhouse, P., and Deakin, R. (1994). *Breathing Life into Training: A Model of Integrated Training*. Melbourne: National Automotive Industry Training Board.

69. Senge, P. (1990). *The Fifth Discipline: The Art and Practice of the Learning Organisation*. New York: Doubleday.　*18, 42, 48–49, 69*

Simon, B. (1960) *Studies in the History of Education 1780 – 1870*. London: Lawrence and Wishart.

119. Stein, S. (1993). *Continuous Learning for Continuous Improvement or Basic Skills, Worker Empowerment and High Performance Organisations: Why You Can't Have One Without the Other*. Conference paper, Bridging the Skills Gap: Quality Connections in the Workplace. Dallas: Texas Consortium for Worker Education.

50. Stein, S. G. (1991) *Workplace Literacy and the Transformation of the American Workplace: A Model for Effective Practice*. Montreal: Paper presented at the Annual Meeting of the American Association for Adult and Continuing Education.

Sticht, T. G. (1991). *Functional Context Education: Learning for and in the world of work*. New York: Ford Foundation.

Sticht, T. G. (1995). *The Military Experience and Workplace Literacy*. Philadelphia: National Centre on Adult Literacy.

Sticht, T., McDonald, B. and Hule, C. (1992). *Getting WELL: Workforce Education and Lifelong Learning*. San Diego: Applied Behavioural and Cognitive Sciences Inc.

51. Sticht, T. G. and Mikulecky, L. (1984). *Job-Related Basic Skills: Cases and Conclusions*. Ohio: National Center for Research in Vocational Education.

52. Street, B. (1984). *Literacy in Theory and Practice*. Cambridge: Cambridge University Press.　*73–77, 83*

Street, B. (1997). *Adult Literacy in the United Kingdom: A History of Research and Practice*. Lancaster: Research and Practice in Adult Literacy (RAPAL).　*12*

Sungaila, H. (1994). Education, Work, and Training: A Post Modernist Thought. *The Workplace in Education* Rydalmere: Edward Arnold Australia.

Sutton, A. (1996). Training and Assessment-Potential Barriers to Workers Accessing National Qualifications. *People and Performance*, (P.38–41). Auckland:

Sweet, M. E. (1984). *Education and Training for Working Life, Leisure, and Unemployment.* (MA dissertation) Coventry: Warwick University.

Taylor, M., Lewe, G. and Draper, J. Eds. (1991). *Basic Skills for the Workplace*. Toronto: Culture Concepts.

Thompson, E. P. (1963). *The Making of the English Working Class*. Harmondsworth: Penguin.   *15*

53. Thompson, P. and McHugh, D. (1990). *Work Organisations*. London: MacMillan Press.   *18, 21*

Toch, T. (1991). *In the Name of Excellence*. New York: Oxford University Press.   *1, 4–6*

54. Toms, J. (1995). Competency-Based Training: Methodology or Ideology? A Critical Approach. *Critical Forum*, 4 (2) Leichhardt: ALBSAC.   *52, 58, 65, 67, 69–70*

106. Trades Union Congress. (1989). *Skills 2000*. London: Congress House.

Trades Union Congress. (1991). *Towards 2000: A consultative Document*. London: Congress House.

107. Trades Union Congress. (1993). *Working in Partnership for Quality Training*. London: Congress House.

Trades Union Congress. (1994). *A New Partnership for Company Training*. London: Congress House.

85. Tuckett, A. (1991). *Towards a Learning Workforce*. Leicester: NIACE.   *58*

Turk, J. (1990). *Literacy: Defining the Problem, Posing the Solution*. Conference paper, Halifax: Canadian Vocational Association.   *36–37*

Turk, J. and Unda, J. (1991). So We Can Make Our Voices Heard: The Ontario Federation of Labor's BEST project on Worker Literacy. In Taylor, M., Lewe, G., and Draper, J. Eds. *Basic Skills for the Workplace* Toronto: Culture Concepts.   *83*

90. Department of Trade and Industry. (1993). *Competitiveness. Helping Businesses to Win*. London: Government Policy Document. HMSO. CM2563.

96. UNESCO. (1976). *The Experimental World Literacy Programme: A Critical Assessment*. Paris: UNESCO Press.

UNESCO. (1978). Revised Recommendation Concerning the International Standardisation of Educational Statistics. Paris: UNESCO.

United States Congress. (1994) Goals 2000: Educate America Act.

United States Congress Office of Technology Assessment (1993). *Adult Literacy and New Technologies: Tools for a Lifetime*. Washington DC: US Government Printing Office

120. US Department of Education. (1992). *Workplace Education: Voices From the Field* Highlands, Massachusetts: Evaluation Research.

55. Velde, C., and Svensson, L. (1996). *The Conception of Competence in Relation to Learning Processes and Change at Work*. Conference paper. Learning and Research in Working Life. Steyr, Austria.   *67*

56. Watkins. P. (1991). *Knowledge and Control in the Flexible Workplace. Geelong, Victoria: Deakin University Press.*

97. Weiner, G. (1990). *Creating a Learning Culture: Work and Literacy in the Nineties*. Ottawa: National Literacy Secretariat.

86. Wickert, R. (1989). *No Single Measure: A Survey of Australian Adult Literacy*. Sydney:

Institute of Technical and Adult Teacher Education, Sydney College of Advanced Education.   *20, 33, 74*

70. Wiggenhorn, W. (1990). Motorola U: When Training Becomes Education. *Harvard Business Review.* (July-August).   *5, 27, 31–32, 47*

Wilkinson, S. (1994). *Quality and Workplace Education: A Guide for Practitioners.* Edinburgh: Scottish Community Education Council.   *47*

Woodruffe, C. (1991). Competent By Any Other Name. *Personnel Management.* (Sept). London: Institute of Personnel Management.   *66*

World Economic Forum. (1989). *World Competitiveness Report .* World Economic Forum and the IMEDE.

Wright, S. (1994). 'It's a Job': Learning in a Public Service Office. *Issues in Work-Related Education.* Adelaide: Deakin University.   *69*

71. Young, C. (1992). Workplace Reform: So Much To Gain. *New Zealand Business.* Auckland: NZ Business Journal.   *48, 60*

Zacharias-Jutz, J. (1993). Workers' Education, Social Reconstruction, and Adult Education. *Adult Education Quarterly*, 43 (2)   *76*

Zuboff, S. (1988). *In the Age of the Smart Machine.* New York: Basic Books.   *39*